I0649194

Frederick Bartlett Goddard

Giving and getting credit : a book for business men

Frederick Bartlett Goddard

Giving and getting credit : a book for business men

ISBN/EAN: 9783337215750

Printed in Europe, USA, Canada, Australia, Japan

Cover: Foto ©Andreas Hilbeck / pixelio.de

More available books at **www.hansebooks.com**

GIVING AND GETTING CREDIT

A BOOK FOR BUSINESS MEN

BY

FREDERICK B. GODDARD

NEW YORK

F. TENNYSON NEELY

114 FIFTH AVENUE

1898

CONTENTS.

CHAPTER I.

CREDIT AND MONEY.

CHAPTER II.

OF FAILURES AND CHANGES IN BUSINESS CONDITIONS.

CHAPTER III.

SUGGESTIONS AND PRECAUTIONS.

CHAPTER VI.

Collection.

CHAPTER VII.

Corporations.

CHAPTER VIII.

The Mercantile Agency System.

CHAPTER XII.

THE PANIC OF 1893.

APPENDIX.

GIVING AND GETTING CREDIT.

CHAPTER I.

CREDIT AND MONEY.

COMMERCIAL credit is the name of that trust which is reposed in men because of their character and resources. In other words, it is an estimate of ability and disposition to fulfil business engagements which confers purchasing power; power to command the industry or the capital of others.

Credit is the opposite of money, for it pays nothing. Debt is a thing to be paid, and money is the thing that pays. But the value which is attached to a merchant's word, the skill and experience he has acquired, and the relations he has established, must surely be considered, in some sense, as capital.

The man who buys with money uses the realized profits of the past. If he buys upon credit, he utilizes the present value of a future payment. He promises to pay a sum of money, and gives the creditor a right of action against him if he fails to pay; this is the legal basis of credit. If, by the lapse of time, or a bankrupt law, he is legally discharged, the obligation is not thereby extinguished; the creditor is merely denied the use of the law to enforce his claim.

Credit neither creates nor destroys capital; it merely transfers to the debtor the property of the creditor, and one is plus only by as much as the other is minus.

If, for example, five men buy from each other, consecutively, a thousand dollars' worth of goods, and each gets the note he receives discounted, five thousand dollars are thus brought into circulation, but no new value is created. If the last purchaser fails to pay his note, and none has surplus capital, the loss of a thousand dollars must run along the line, and each becomes bankrupt. Yet the goods may still exist, and, except in the confusion and distress which follow, the community is neither richer nor poorer than before.

This is the condition of affairs when credit becomes too much expanded and the crash of widespread bankruptcy sponges the slate. It shows that the credit system is a vast series of mutual dependencies, and that the solvency of merchants rests largely upon that of their neighbors.

Credit is a tax upon labor, because prices on credit are higher than for cash. Those who take credit and pay, are charged to make up average losses from those who do not pay. The good insure the bad, so to speak, and cash discounts show the cost of credit.

No one becomes bankrupt who does not owe. Credit is, therefore, a cause of bankruptcies.

Credit favors extravagance and speculation. It is easy to spend or risk money which has cost neither labor nor self-denial, but merely a promise to pay hereafter. Social economists say that a family which buys its supplies on credit spends much more than if it pays cash. Credit stimulates demand and raises prices, yet it is a blessing to the sick or unemployed workman, because it enables him to draw upon the future for his necessities.

Credit pays capital for permitting itself to be employed in reproduction, and transfers it from hands that cannot use it into hands that can. It enables those who have industry but no capital to enjoy the advantages of both, and leads it into channels through which commodities are moved over the civilized world from producer to consumer.

Without credit, the present business of the world could not be transacted. Not all the gold ever taken from the earth could perform its service.

It constructs railways, opens mines, improves farms, and builds houses: it is "the soul of commerce," an agent and promoter of civilization wherever human energies can be exerted.

Credit is the fruit of a settled condition and was therefore unknown in the early stages of society. It has succeeded the primitive periods of barter and money, or cash, and appears only when the observance of contracts is enforced by public authority. Wise and beneficent credit follows the largest personal liberty, but is opposed to every form of misrule and anarchy,

and flourishes best under the wing of strong
and secure government.

It is estimated that from ninety to ninety-five
per cent of the world's present business is transacted upon credit. Daniel Webster declared
that "credit has done more a thousand times to
enrich nations than all the mines of all the
world."

Real or metallic money, coined by public authority, is the standard measure of values which
denotes and carries in itself an exchangeable
value equal to that of the average quantity of
labor required to mine and coin its metal. It
is therefore not only a measurer and medium of
exchange, but an object of exchange, like other
products of labor and capital.

It is this intrinsic property which insures absolute confidence in it, without which there is
sure to be confusion and distress. One of the
chief causes of the panic of 1893 was that while
gold and silver were equal in legal-tender qualities, their relative value was unstable.[1]

---

[1] Silver dollars are an unlimited legal tender in the
United States. In Great Britain silver is a legal tender
for forty shillings. A legal-tender dollar contains 412½

The price of a thing, which is its trade or commercial value, may fluctuate according to demand and supply; money is also subject to constant oscillations between plenty and scarcity, but it is supposed to stand still while prices of other things move. As a gold dollar is a unit of value, we cannot think of it as worth more or less than a dollar. 'Its pulsations of commercial value are not registered in itself, but in the prices of staple commodities; increase their supply and they become cheaper; increase the relative quantity of money and they tend to rise in price. If business stagnates, less money is needed; consequently it becomes more abundant, with an easy rate of interest, which encourages enterprise and advancing prices.

Money is also a token of credit for labor per-

---

grains of standard silver. The faith of the Government is pledged to maintain its current parity with gold. The "free silver" advocates desire that the Government shall coin all the silver offered by any person, at the ratio of sixteen to one with gold.

The Act of June 9th, 1879, provided that the subsidiary silver coin of the United States should be legal tender in all sums not exceeding ten dollars. Five-cent nickel pieces are legal tender to the amount of 25 cents; one-cent pieces to the amount of 4 cents.

formed. Bastiat says, "Money is, in effect, an order to pay to bearer a service equal to that which he has rendered mankind." Burke called gold and silver "the two great recognized species that represent the conventional credit of mankind."

Paper money is merely a promise to pay in metallic money. Coin money is the standard, paper money the instrument. Being more convenient, it is seldom converted into coin unless the holder becomes alarmed.

Perhaps the wealthy actually handle less money than the poorer classes, because they deal chiefly by credits. They exchange the title to money. They deposit checks in bank and draw checks upon it. The principal function of the bank is to transfer credits from one account to another, and it neither receives nor pays out much cash, relatively to the amount of its transactions. It has been said that the bulk of current money is used by those who are too poor or too little known to obtain or to utilize credit.

Proportionally less money is now required to transact the world's vastly increased volume of business, because it has been so generally

2

superseded by credit, with its implements or machinery. But credit must rest upon some substantial foundation, some absolute, stable measure and representative of value, and to furnish this is, in these days, the chief function of money.

As confidence, so essential to credit, is best assured where personal and property rights are most secure, there is the highest civilization; there also is the largest variety of pursuits; money and credit are most active, and the rate of interest lowest. There, therefore, is the greatest demand for labor and the most abundant production.

Credit is practically the rule in wholesale transactions throughout the world, while money passes chiefly in retail trading, or in payment for labor. It is obvious that the abolition of credit would mean a vastly increased demand for money.

It is to be noted, however, that while time transactions may still maintain their relative proportion in general wholesale business, the credit system is undergoing certain important modifications. During the last few years there has been a great decline in the price of most commodities, and to secure former profits a larger bulk of goods must be handled. Increasing competition adds to the cost of effecting sales, while it also decreases percentages of profit. Under these circumstances manufacturers and merchants find it necessary to eliminate risk as much as possible from their dealings; hence the large discounts offered for cash, and an increasing desire to curtail the length of credits.

Industry, like climate, has its seed-time and harvest, and the consumption of its annual products has its natural progression and its periodic completion. The distribution of these products under the credit system should properly conform to this natural order of production and consumption. So, also, shorter credits should follow improved transportation, because goods pass more quickly from producer to consumer. But, in fact, long credits are given rather as a temptation to the purchaser than as a requirement of natural conditions.

Every debt implies a credit, and all the debts are equal to all the credits. Debts for merchandise are extinguished by selling that merchandise and applying to them the proceeds. Men buy and give promises to pay, they sell and take promises to pay, and their capital or credit enables them to stand in the gap and apply those they take to those they give. It virtually requires all the credits to pay all the debts.

Experience shows that, during a generally prosperous condition of affairs, credit is expanded until a fever of speculation culminates, and debts are incurred by "booming" towns, building railways, and similar projects. But when the mercantile community has been seduced into devoting any considerable proportion of its credits to purposes outside its natural channels, the process of adjustment is deranged and confidence gives way to distrust with its train of evils. Our periodical panics have in fact been born less of adversity than of the abuse of prosperity.

Again; it is impossible that the entire debts of a community could be paid at once. The ability to pay depends on the gradual and regular manner in which they mature, and the amounts paid to-day render possible to the

business world its payments of to-morrow.
Each line of trade establishes for itself its customary terms of credit. If it were the general
custom to extend a credit of four months to
purchasers in the boot and shoe trade, for instance, and a material quantity of intermediate
credits of eight months be granted, a link is
broken in the chain.

Bankers complain that "an adequate supply
of business paper is yearly becoming more difficult to obtain." Some trades, notably those
which deal in staple products, the rubber, the
jewelry, and a few other lines, still largely retain the old-fashioned system of settlement by
notes; but merchandise is now chiefly sold on
open account. So common has this practice
become that the offer of a bunch of small notes,
as bills receivable, for discount, is sometimes
held by bankers to signify a "needy condition."

At least two-thirds of all the paper bought
by banks and capitalists in New York is
"single name" paper. It is generally preferred
by them to "double name" paper, because the
simple and direct promise to pay of a concern
whose character and resources are known and

approved, is deemed safer than a shared responsibility which may introduce some devious feature of accommodation for both maker and
indorser.[1]

It is no longer considered "kiting" for houses
in good credit to sell their notes, and with the
avails secure cash discounts on purchases. It
is even currently said that if, in ordinary years,
merchants in some lines of trade cannot float
their single name paper and buy for cash, they
are "undesirable as customers." But there are
many concerns which enjoy excellent credit in
mercantile circles, whose paper cannot be sold
to banks and capitalists, because it is not known
to the note-brokers.

An enormous volume of paper is kept afloat
by some large houses, and they cannot afford to
withdraw their names from the street, even
though they have no use for the money. Credit
unused grows rusty. "It is now," says a

---

[1] M. Leon Say avers that the best form of credit for
banking purposes is purely personal credit: "Le
crédit tout court sans phrase. Le crédit sur gage n'a
jamais été que l'enfance du crédit. Le crédit public
n'existait quand les rois empruntaient sur leurs reliques
ou sur les bijoux."

banker, "a prevalent idea among merchants that a concern which does not place its paper in the open market, or use bank facilities, is not in first-class credit."[1]

Chartered trust companies and savings banks are forbidden by law to loan on single name paper; large amounts are, however, passed into loans by some of these institutions, through brokers, with "straw" indorsements. National banks are not thus restricted.

There are some who think that later on, in accordance with specialization, or the division of labor principle, the special and peculiar concern of the manufacturer will be more to fabricate, and of the merchant to distribute, and that the credit of both will increasingly centre in the banker. In other words, it may become still more his function to measure the responsibility of the others and supply them with cash for their dealings. But it is unlikely that any

---

[1] It will be understood that the movement of commercial affairs under exceptional conditions, such as have existed during the present business depression, may not indicate their general drift or tendency. "All signs fail in dry weather."

system will ever prevail extensively which brings a financial intermediary between the simple and natural credit relations of buyer and seller, unless under some form of guarantee.

Nor is the banker, as a rule, as well qualified by circumstances to estimate the responsibility of an applicant for credit as the man from whom he buys his goods. It is an old saying in the business world that "if you wish to know anything about a bank's customer, don't ask the bank." The merchant's relations with his customer are closer. He knows whether he is a prudent buyer and a good business man, and his ledger account shows the degree of promptness with which he has met his payments and the manner of his dealing. All this knowledge the banker can only obtain at second-hand.

Aside from the fact that there is less risk in granting a short credit than a long one, there is also more profit in the nimble sixpence, or the more frequent turning-over of capital. It is interesting to see the figures; for example, a thousand dollars turned over once each year with accrued profits, for five years, reckoning the profit on each investment or sale at twenty per cent. will give an aggregate of $2,488.32. The same sum turned over *twice* each year, for five years, under the same conditions, will amount to $6,191.74; and *three* times yearly to $15,407.02; in another year, or in *six* years, the thousand dollars will, under the same conditions, if turned over *three* times yearly, aggregate $26,623.33 as against but $8,916.10, if invested but *twice* a year.

CHAPTER II.

OF FAILURES AND CHANGES IN BUSINESS CONDITIONS.

ON the Canton River numbers of people live in house-boats, or sampans, and raise water-fowl, which are taught, upon a signal, to scurry home to the boat as fast as possible. But some one of the ducks and geese must be the last to get in, and that unfortunate is always punished. And so among business men; some failures will surely occur because it is not in the nature of things that all can succeed. All in trade are liable to casualties and reverses which imply no crime, and which the average sagacity can neither forecast nor avert.

And there appears to be as practical uniformity in the number of business failures, proportioned to the "business population," in a series of years, as in the social phenomena of mar-

riages, births, deaths, suicides, etc., in proportion to the general population.[1]

There is much disparity in the proportion of
losses by bad debts in the various kinds of business, and it is difficult to obtain facts upon
which to base calculations of the average percentage of net loss on the *total* volume of credit
sales of merchandise. Some estimates have
placed it as high as $\frac{8.5}{100}$ of one per cent, others
as low as $\frac{40}{100}$ of one per cent. Probably it lies
somewhere in the mean, but we shall never
know how near we are to the truth of the matter until we have reliable data upon which to
generalize and reckon. We do know, however,
that about one concern in ninety fails annually,
on the average, and statistics show also the aggregate liabilities of all failed concerns and their
assets.

A French economist reckons that ten out of
every hundred who enter business succeed, fifty
vegetate, and forty become bankrupt. It has
been lately calculated that in the United States

---

[1] The expectation of everywhere discovering regularity
in the midst of confusion has now become an article of
faith with the most eminent scientific men.

ninety-five per cent of the business men "fail
to succeed." Things in business go chiefly by
law, and not by luck; the fittest only survive,
and at least eighty per cent of those who fail,
with liabilities exceeding assets, can find in
themselves the causes of their failure.

The Mercantile Agency approximates the
total number of commercial failures in the
United States during the last thirty-eight years,
or from 1857 to 1894 inclusive, at 252,524, with
liabilities amounting, in round numbers, to $5,-
500,000,000. These constant losses have fallen
upon the mercantile community sometimes as
noiselessly as snowflakes, and again fitfully, in
gusts and swirls. Some idea may perhaps be
had of the amount of new business necessary to
be transacted in order to retrieve them.

Such an aggregate gives one a feeling of respect for that cautious and thoughtful Dutch-
man, who sold his goods lower on credit than
for cash, in order to cut down his risk from bad
debts. These figures show the average liabilities of each failure to be about $20,000.

No data is obtainable to show, even with ap-
proximate accuracy, what proportion of this

vast sum was finally paid to creditors, or what relation it bears to the total volume of business transacted upon credit during this period. These and many kindred statistical facts, carefully gathered, analyzed, and considered in their relation to currency, tariffs, and other varying political and financial conditions, would certainly be of practical benefit to the business world and useful to public men, as a basis for induction to great and guiding principles.

The history of commercial affairs during the last fifty or sixty years demonstrates that business in the United States has three phases, viz., prosperity, panic, and reorganization, or liquidation and settlement, and that we have been relatively prosperous about three-quarters of the time. There seems to be a rhythmic oscillation toward a period of extreme depression about every tenth or twelfth year.

These facts are suggestive. There are times when a prudent merchant will take warning from the past; seasons when he should be advised that a panic is "due." Again, after a panic, when the liquidation has been radical and complete, he may reasonably expect a period of comparative safety for expanding enterprise.

It is often asserted that, in credit dealings, a poor man who is honest is safer than a richer one whose good faith is not assured. Certainly, men possessing a talent for business can often largely increase the energy and effectiveness of even a small capital and come safely off. Captains like Napoleon have led a handful of soldiers to victory against overmatching battalions, and many a poor man with superior qualities has struggled against great odds to the very front rank of fortune and credit; and many more will do so.

But Mercantile Agency returns show that, in recent years, downright dishonesty is a less important factor in mercantile losses than "lack of capital and capacity," which are held to account for about "three-fifths of the total number of business failures, and three-quarters of the aggregate liabilities." Too many are like Artemus Ward when he "tried to do too much and did it."

Therefore simple probity, which means proved honesty, while a great strengthener of confidence, cannot be generally accepted as a sufficient basis for extensive credit. It is evident that capital and capacity should also be cardinal considerations.

A man with tangible means has a hostage in sight. His property is, in a manner, collateral security that he can and must fulfil his engagements. The first steps to wealth are difficult; its accumulation implies sagacity, experience, and thrift, or the valuable habit of saving, and its owner usually becomes more cautious and conservative than one who has no capital to lose. Cynical observers say that men in comfortable circumstances are also less liable to do crooked things than those who are pinched for money, because they are less tempted.

Those who with a large capital do an unsafely large business are proportionately less numerous than those who carry too much sail on a limited, or small, capital, and they are apt to be in a relatively better position to secure quicker and stronger support in time of need than the smaller concerns. Changed and changing business conditions render it constantly more difficult to succeed, without sufficient

capital and business aptitude, and they tend
also to limit losses by hastening, as never before, the almost inevitable catastrophe.

Steam and electricity have changed the relations of men.[1] The range of affairs to be over-
seen is immensely widened. We are now in
quick touch with all the world, and every im-

---

[1] It is stated as a significant instance of economic progress that the works at Niagara Falls will, when completed, furnish and distribute as electricity "an amount
of power available for manufacturing purposes, equal-
ling, if not exceeding, the aggregate amount of steam
and water power in use in all industries in the United
States as reported by the census of 1880." The passing
age of steam bequeathes to us the coming age of electricity, and probably the dreams of to-day will be the
substantial realities of to-morrow.

In a recent issue of *The North American Review*, the
English statistician and political economist, Professor
Mulhall, says: "If we take a survey of mankind in ancient or modern times as regards the physical, mechanical and intellectual force of nations, we find nothing
to compare with the United States in this present year
of 1895. At the same time we see that the wealth of
the American people surpasses that of any other nation,
past or present. . . . The United States in 1895 possesses
by far the greatest productive power in the world; this
power has more than trebled since 1860; the intellectual
progress of the nation is attended to in a more liberal
manner than in Europe, and the accumulation of wealth
averages $7,000,000 daily."

provement in communication and transportation, and each labor-saving invention, adds to the delicacy of trade calculations. Prices fluctuate within narrower limits then formerly, but the element of speculation is still a factor to be considered in manufacture or importation. New facilities sweep by old ones and distance them, and possibility of invention, labor conditions, demand, and competition are all constantly more uncertain. A single mistake, or misadventure, may sweep away the enterprising man with small capital.

And there is a curious disproportion between causes and effects, which is natural perhaps, because the public imagination is whimsical and not governed in its conclusions by laws like those which control ants and bees. A great astronomer said, he could calculate the motions of erratic stars, but not the opinions of men. For example, an event logically calculated to produce a certain movement of prices upon the exchange, appears often to affect them in an opposite and most unexpected manner.

If harvests are scanty, the products may sell for more than if they were abundant; a small

3

crop often brings more than a large one; and when abundant the price may decline so that less can be realized upon the whole product by an amount many times the value of the surplus. And so in many things. The most sagacious must often grope their way, because at times future events and prices can as little be conjectured as if they depended wholly on chance.

Yet, after all, in intricate and perplexing conditions the advantage remains with the master mind. And it is a corollary of the growth of such conditions in industrial pursuits that a constantly increasing tribute is paid to superior business ability and training.

In earlier and simpler, and perhaps happier, times, creditors and debtors came nearer together. Merchants and customers became friends; they looked into each others' eyes and discussed resources, advantages, and prospects. But in late years, this pleasant and beneficial contact has become less frequent. We have no personal acquaintance with a large proportion of the people we deal with.

In the complex march of modern affairs, business has become more mechanical. We deal less with men than with things. We have lost the personal equation of our customers, or get it only at second-hand. The name of a debtor or creditor on our books is only a symbol which might as well be represented by a number.

This transition has reached even local lines of business. One of the largest livery-stable proprietors in New York says that ten years ago he knew all his customers personally, while now he practically knows none of them, all his business being transacted through the labor-saving telephone.

Thus intuitions, personal knowledge of human nature, and judgment of individual character can be no longer accounted as helpful factors in determining credit, in the majority of cases. The trader is also deprived of the personal interest and counsel of the merchant, and if disaster overtakes him he has none of the regrets of friendship for the losses of a man whom he never knew. His honor becomes an abstract sentiment without the strengthening of a social compact, and his course is more liable to be swayed by the fitful winds of his own personal advantage.

But there are also compensations in modern progress. It has multiplied sources of information in regard to men and their affairs, so that their home reputation, resources, and the manner of their dealing can easily and quickly be known. The knave can no longer hide himself; the shadow of a fraudulent failure follows him to the remotest village or cross-road, and his unsavory record confronts him whenever and wherever he again asks credit. Nor can he who has shown himself incapable or negligent when entrusted with the property of others, altogether conceal the facts. He must show that he has gained wisdom and prudence before he will be held as again entitled to substantial confidence and credit.

On the other hand, he who is overwhelmed through no fraud or folly of his own, finds his record for probity and ability an unforgotten and helpful force to put him again upon his feet. Yet it must be confessed that poverty often seems to get more punishment than crime. We have all seen men whose "debts were the only measure of their profits," and who flourish on fraud. They fail, force a compromise, and with their booty start afresh. They ride while their creditors travel afoot.[1]

We have also seen cases where men have made an unfortunate rather than a fraudulent failure, and who, after giving up all and struggling for years to obtain another footing, have finally gone into hopeless oblivion. They could obtain no credit because they were destitute, and remained destitute because they could obtain no credit.

These causes are often pitiable. To feel honest poverty is bad enough, but there is a deeper

---

[1] A thief who had grown gray in the exercise of his profession at length declared himself warmly in favor of the proposition that "Honesty is the best policy." The reasons he gave for his conversion were substantially as follows: He had known two crooks who became tired of doing time in prison, and they agreed with each other that when they got out they would be "honest." So, upon their release, they went to another city and began a legitimate business. By dint of industry and promptness in meeting their obligations they prospered, and at length built up such a credit that they succeeded in obtaining merchandise to the value of a hundred thousand dollars! Then they sold the goods and skipped out with the proceeds.

"They couldn't have done it," said the old thief, "if they hadn't been honest."

pang when we are made to realize that we have
not sufficient merit to retrieve our circumstances, and that the world has hopelessly forgotten us.   But in such a state of affairs, as
Mr. Lincoln said of himself during the darkest
days of the War, we "need success rather than
sympathy."

It will generally be found, however, that in
the latter class of cases there is a deficiency of
pluck, energy, or balance, and in the former,
that the perpetrators of such frauds possess
qualities which would have ensured to them a
greater degree of prosperity, had they been honest and avoided the stigma of dishonorable failure.   Observation and experience teach prudent merchants that one successful crime sooner
or later invites to the commission of another,
and they cannot afford to forget.   It is a clumsy
rogue who, in these days, fails, in order to
make money.   He cannot cover his tracks.
There are smoother paths of robbery.

When the year's bad debts are charged off to
profit and loss, the merchant may console himself with the thought that the lessons he has
learned will make him more cautious in the

future. He thinks that experience has satu-
rated him with wisdom. But experience has
been likened to the stern-lights of a ship, which
illuminate only the path it has gone over. The
conditions of yesterday never return; dealings
with one have little prophetic value in dealing
with another; the next loss may come under
totally different circumstances, and from a
direction entirely unsuspected.

Human activities present such a tangled coil;
character and conditions vary so greatly, that
particular decisions respecting men and their
affairs have no universal application. All losses
are exceptional. We never sell goods that we
do not expect to be paid for. It is the unexpected which makes bad debts.

As confusion sometimes exists in regard to
the meaning of the words Insolvency, Failure,
and Bankruptcy, it may be well to define them.
Insolvency is a state, or condition; Failure an
act flowing out of that state; Bankruptcy the
effect of that act. A man who is insolvent cannot pay his debts in full; one who fails ceases
to pay. The bankrupt is strictly a trader who
is "bank broken," and who legally surrenders

his property into the hands of his creditors. Bankruptcy is a legal act which dissolves the firm. Insolvency signifies more than bankruptcy. A concern may fail and become bankrupt and yet not be insolvent, for the estate may pay in full; and many a man who, if pressed to liquidate, would be found solvent only as snow in the sun is solvent, may never fail or become bankrupt.[1]

---

[1] An insolvent law is essentially a law by which a debtor is exempted from liability to arrest or imprisonment for debt previously contracted, on condition of his delivering up all his property for the benefit of his creditors.

Distinctions between bankruptcy and insolvency have been practically abandoned in this country, yet enactments of State legislatures for the relief of debtors are still called insolvent laws, those of the General Government bankrupt laws.

Chief Justice Marshall says: "A bankrupt law may contain those regulations which are generally found in insolvent laws, and an insolvent law may contain those which are common to a bankrupt law."

CHAPTER III.

INTELLIGENT business men now broadly recognize that both the ethics and the policy of trade require them to make known their financial position. It is a practice to be encouraged, because, as it becomes general, it tends to suppress blind and undeserved credit risks which so often lead to irritating losses, while it helps to fortify the business world against panics, by giving it more exact knowledge of debtors' resources, and therefore greater confidence and stability.

A man in good circumstances who refuses to reveal his condition renders it impossible for his banker, his references, or the mercantile agencies to speak with certainty in regard to his affairs. His reticence may naturally raise doubt and indirect inquiry, and it generally deprives him, in some measure, of that valuable confidence and credit which he might otherwise be justified in expecting. Nor can he as surely and quickly obtain financial help in time of need if his resources are unknown or merely conjectured.

A prominent New York bank official, of long experience, asserts that "an applicant for credit should be willing to make a full and frank showing in writing over his signature, and if he declines to do so, I believe that we should give no consideration to his application for discount. After gathering careful statistics on the subject, I have reached the conclusion that when a borrower refuses absolutely to give any information in this way, his credit is impaired and it is only a question of time when misfortune will overtake him. There is no concern that does any amount of business that at some time in its history does not need the help, confidence, and co-operation of its bank, and nothing should be concealed from it."

In a recent address before the Illinois Bankers' Association, Hon. S. S. Lacy, ex-Comptroller of the Currency, and president of the Bankers' National Bank of Chicago, said:

"The age of mystery as related to business affairs is happily passing away. The time was when business men considered it akin to an insult to be called upon, when asking credit, for a statement of their affairs. Fortunately wiser and sounder views now prevail, and no right-minded man or well-managed institution now hesitates, when asking favors, to place the prospective creditor in full possession of the facts upon which credits can be intelligently extended."

In February last (1895), the Executive Council of the New York State Bankers' Association passed a resolution recommending to banks throughout the State the procuring from borrowers of written statements showing their assets and liabilities. It was asserted that if this measure were generally adopted by banks and bankers, they could act with more adequate knowledge, and therefore with greater security, and that it would also, in effect, "eliminate from the mercantile community borrowers whose standing and credit are now a menace to reputable merchants."

It is certainly a sound business principle that

he who is asked for credit is justified in making the applicant prove that he is worthy of it, and that the latter is bound to furnish forth all essential facts in aid of the investigation which he virtually challenges.

This principle would be insisted upon universally by merchants if sellers were as much in demand as buyers, and could afford to be as independent. But competition is keen, and all are eager to sell goods, to keep things moving, and to reap profits. The buyer generally holds the honors, and rules are apt to bow before him as "nice customs courtesy to great kings."

If an applicant for mercantile credit declines to answer reasonable inquiries, or is restive under them, it is a natural inference, but not always a certain conclusion, that he wishes to conceal something unfavorable. He may be eccentric, and yet solvent and prompt of pay. He may object from pride or from prejudice. He is, perhaps, unreasonably sensitive about having his credit investigated. He may be reluctant to make known, not how poor, but how rich he is. Possibly he is mindful of the income tax, or shy on account of his property taxes. There are responsible men who appear to regard interrogatories in regard to their affairs as so many impertinent conundrums. Others assume that it implies ignorance not to know their standing, and affect to be irritated when it is questioned. And there are some, reticent by nature, who believe in a "still hunt."

But the real thing is not as likely to be mistaken for a sham, as a sham for the real thing; and the cranky, reticent man is never as dangerous as the plausible rogue who can prove as much as anybody will believe.[1]

Nature sometimes withholds stability, judgment and effectiveness from a man, and by way of compensation endows him with a most plausible tongue. But if the applicant for credit, as Hamlet says, "doth protest too much," it operates to put a sagacious merchant on guard. Nor, on the other hand, will he often let a good but buttoned-up customer slip through his fingers, because he cannot learn that he is responsible.

---

[1] The United States Commissioner of Labor, Carroll D. Wright, who knows all about statistics, puts it that "figures will not lie, but liars will figure."

The logic of business requires that capital should be kept as active as its safe and legitimate employment will permit. Except as a safety reserve there should no more be idle dollars than idle clerks. Facilities for obtaining information are abundant, and he who neglects to provide himself with them either takes blind risks, or limits his business and narrows his profits.

Men in trade sometimes say, "I don't care about my credit, I buy for cash," forgetting that a great advantage of the capitalist is not altogether his hard cash, but the credit his capital commands, which many times multiplies its producing power. Many a concern has failed because it neglected to establish credit when it was not needed, that it might be available in time of need.

Chances are often knowingly taken with old patrons which would not for a moment be considered from new applicants for credit. We are more the creatures of habit than we realize, and the risks we are familiar with are apt to be minimized against our better judgment, by long intercourse and safe dealing. This is natural and kindly, but in business it is weak. The unlucky passengers are those who are on board when the ship goes down.

A merchant's ledger is his barometer, so to speak; it often indicates that a storm is gathering. If a customer's account is analyzed and it is found that two years ago he discounted his bills, that last year he grew tardy in his payments, that he pleads for "dating," and is slower still this year, there is some reason for it. Is he doing too much business for his capital? This can be ascertained. Has he lost his money? If not, it is surely not in the right place. In either case it is time for the merchant to take careful bearings and perhaps shorten sail.

Prudence and precaution surely do not conflict with the Golden Rule, neither do they imply truth in the popular but atrocious maxim that there should be "no friendship in business." It is true that sharp competition is not a nourisher of sentiment and that principle is better than feeling. Damon and Pythias have become rivals in the race for money, and *fin de siècle* friendship is apt to be more a matter of calculation than of emotion.

Yet withal, keeping in mind Thoreau's *bon mot*, "Good heart, weak head," cordial and friendly relations are quite compatible with strict business principles and mutually beneficial. Trade would become a dismal and depressing pursuit indeed, if all kindly, disinterested, and generous sentiments were to be banithed from it.

Admitting that, in a large and general way, there is a law of average losses from bad debts, it can have no bearing upon individual risks, because each has peculiar circumstances which call for the exercise of special scrutiny. Giving credits upon the chance that only a certain percentage will turn out badly is like shooting without aim.

As eternal vigilance is the price of liberty, so also it is the price of success in giving credit. It does not follow that because a man has paid many times he will pay again. Argus eyes have time and again warded off serious losses by discovering signals of "dry rot," or of distress, in concerns whose solvency was not questioned in the community. The wisdom of fifty men is not the wisdom of one multiplied by

fifty.   If the one is alert enough to discover new
and leading facts, he may have a clearer vision
than all the rest.   A failure seldom occurs that
some one does not get an inkling of it beforehand.

The majority of men prefer to be, and mean
to be, honest, but it is natural to be hopeful and
to present the most sanguine view of one's own
circumstances and prospects.   The tendency is
to advertise profits and conceal losses.   Men do
not talk of ill luck until near the end of the
struggle.   Rumor usually magnifies wealth and
soon becomes current opinion.   Many walk
about in a popular halo of stocks and bonds
who cannot pay their debts, and the general belief in their mythical possessions enables them
to flourish, at least for a time.   The weakness
of the credit system lies in the fact that a
man's credit depends, not upon his real worth
or property, but upon his reputation for having
it, and he is tempted to puff himself.

Neither common report, good birth, good
clothes, good address, political reputation, fame,
nor evangelical piety, establishes a sufficient
basis for credit.   Men in high station some-
4

times have a hearty contempt for their pecu-
niary obligations. An English nobleman said of
a man, that he had muddled away his fortune
in paying tradesmen's bills; and Pelham argues
that it is respectable to be arrested for debt, because it shows that the party once had credit.
Our business salvation requires that we walk
by facts and not by faith.

Display will not mislead a sensible business
man, neither will excessive liberality. It has
been said that there is perhaps no character so
seldom met with as that of a man who is strictly reasonable in the value he sets on property;
who can be liberal without profusion, and economical without avarice. The chief end of man
is not to accumulate dollars, but the majority
of men cannot pay their honest debts without
being frugal and saving; and those who gratify
themselves when they cannot afford it, do so at
the expense of others. Thrift implies the habit
of sacrificing present enjoyment for future
good.

A good merchant will not permit his confidence to precede knowledge, or his action to
blunder on in the front of thought. He must

be convinced, not merely persuaded, before he will entrust his property to others. He realizes that giving credit implies risk, and also that he is not in business altogether for his health, but to make reasonable ventures for the sake of profit. He will recollect that there is a hundred-fold more good business than bad in the world, and while he makes safety the chief consideration, he will also guard against the weakness of timidity and over-caution. He will be deliberate, but enterprising also and steadfast.

The cost of conducting a business is a highly important consideration; and, as a general rule, expenses do not increase in proportion with the volume of business. A leading Mercantile Agency made some special investigations along this line at the request of a New York bank president. Eleven representative concerns in various lines, doing an annual trade of $109,000,000, showed expenses of $6,925,000, or an average of about 6 1-2 per cent, as follows:

	Expenses Per Cent.
Jobbing hardware, one house	15
Jewelry, one house	15
Steam pumps, one house	15
Railroad supplies and machinery, one house	10

	Expenses Per Cent.
Groceries (no liquors) two houses:	
One house.....................................	6
One house.....................................	6¼
Groceries (with liquor) one house.................	8
Dry goods, jobbing, two houses:	
One with annual business of $40,000,000.......	5½
" " " " " $10,000,000.......	6¼
Commission dry goods, one house, with annual	
business of $10,000,000.......................	1½
Commission woollens, one house.	2½

Similar statistics taken from the statements made direct to the same gentleman by ten leading houses in representative lines of business, show:

Total annual business	$12,693,000
Total expenses	900,000

Percentage of expenses to annual business, a small fraction over 7 per cent, proportioned as follows:

	Per Cent.
Retail dry goods, two houses: One	20
One..............	16.6
Wholesale groceries, two houses; One in New York	3.5
One West.......	5
Wholesale hardware, one house	9
Wholesale clothing, two houses: One............	5.7
One (reputed close and economical)..........	3.6
Wholesale tobacco, two houses: One.......	2
One	4
Manufacturing cigars, one house.................	4.9

The matter of personal expenditure is also worthy of attention, because many failures are due to this item. Extravagant living is even more ruinous than light profits, because, while the former is never relinquished except under compulsion, the latter may improve.

Those who in prosperous and piping times have established stylish social relations find it particularly hard to retrench when business declines and the income is impaired. They sometimes shrink from making known the actual condition of their affairs, even to their own families, and enforcing the necessary economy, so they grow poor, in order to keep up the appearance of being rich.

Some houses have an exhaustive formula of questions prepared, to which satisfactory answers are obtained before a new account will be opened. The paper is then filed away for future reference. The catechism given below is practically the one now in use by a successful house in New York city:

Full name?
Locality?
Age?

Nationality?
Nature of business?
Capital in business?
Capital outside of business?
Volume of business to capital?
Has the business been profitable?
Withdrawals for personal expenses?
Expense of conducting business preceding year?
Nature of the assets?
Liabilities?
Previous dealings with whom?
Who are the principal creditors?
Agency rating?
References?
Past record?
Ever failed?
Ever had a fire?
Married?
Habits?
Ability?
Industry?
Experience?
Punctuality?
Speculative outside?
Insurance?
Partners, general and special?
Family connections?
Contingent liabilities, as indorsements, etc?
Remarks.

Definite and verified answers to all these queries should certainly furnish a basis for positive conclusions.   But not every man whose trade is desirable will permit himself to be led solemnly to the "sweat box" and put through such a formal inquisition.

A man of tact can, however, bring out many of these facts, with clews to other facts, in an easy conversation, and obtain the rest from collateral sources.

A sensible business man, opening an account with strangers, should know, and does know, that they must somehow acquire knowledge of his responsibility. And with such a customer, a courteous and expectant attitude at the proper moment is often the only interrogatory needed to elicit a voluntary statement.

It is only leading and influential houses that can carry much red tape in these days of competition. We can all sit on the fence and order the mountain to come to us, but if it will not come, we go to the mountain. It is easy to make all sorts of rules, but with the great majority of concerns the rule that is never broken is the rule of expediency. "I do not want processes, but results," said Jay Gould.

A travelling salesman has called many times upon a firm, and at last he secures an order out of the very teeth of a dozen fierce competitors.

He is instructed to investigate the standing and character of his customers, but when he begins to propound the usual questions, the buyer says, "Oh, I have no time to go into all that. If you are afraid, you can cancel the order. I can get all the goods I want in a dozen directions." This firm is probably good, and what is the salesman to do? He will do the best he can. He will act, and his house will act, upon collateral information.

CHAPTER IV.

THE most searching and decisive test of a man's actual financial condition is his balance sheet, or statement, signed by himself and fully verified. Other information concerning him may be misconceived, or uncertain, but there is no mistaking such a presentment of his affairs. Nor can he wriggle away from his written statement as he might from his verbal declarations. If it is garbled, if the assets are wilfully placed too high and the liabilities too low, in order to obtain credit favors, or an agency rating, the maker braves the penalty of fraud.

The construction of a statement, or the manner in which it is made up, indicates much as to the business methods of the concern which makes it. 'Some statements are plain, explicit, comprehensive; others vague, confused, and perhaps equivocal.

An ambiguous statement points at one of two conclusions: if it is a frank transcript from the books of the applicant for credit, and does not set forth his condition clearly, he is ignorant in regard to his own affairs. He is not a good business man. On the other hand, if it is a case of *suppressio veri* and *suggestio falsi*, it is a trap.

More than one instance is upon record in recent years where two members of an important firm have made simultaneous statements of its affairs unknown to each other, which varied greatly in essential respects.

The liabilities and receivables of a house are constantly varying quantities, and so also is the relative proportion of cash; a statement made at one season should therefore be considered with relation to the probable position at another. A trader will, for example, appear to be upon a much stronger and more conservative footing after he has made his collections and paid his debts of the past season, than when, a few months later, he is extended between the payables and receivables of the next active season. Large outstandings, in proportion to the amount of business, imply either too liberal credits, or slack collections. And it is generally regarded as against the canons of credit for a merchant to permit any concern to owe him more than twenty or twenty-five per cent of its capital.

In analyzing a statement, special heed should be given to the capital, volume of business, and the average time of credit given, taken in relation to each other. The larger the amount of business, and the longer the credit given, the heavier may naturally be the liabilities of the average concern, while, of course, a small business, with moderate capital, should show but small liabilities.

Two values may be estimated upon every man's estate—one before, and one after failure; and the effects of the contingency should be kept in view. Assets shrink, but liabilities never. Traders' merchandise, and accounts receivable, are said to net, on the average, certainly no more than sixty or sixty-five per cent under the process of winding up for the benefit of creditors; and the manufacturer's machinery and plant but twenty or twenty-five per cent. In fact, machinery, in such cases, is often sold

for old iron.   If, therefore, the assets of an average concern do not considerably exceed its
liabilities, it is really insolvent if compelled to
liquidate; although, if circumstances favor, it
may continue, meeting its engagements, and
gaining financial strength.

As a rule, merchandise is a quick asset at
current value, in proportion to its nearness to
raw material.   That is to say, articles like cotton, wool, leather, iron, rubber, etc., can generally be turned into cash with less delay and loss
than their manufactured products, such as cloth,
garments, shoes, hats, hardware, etc.   In modern times, the more labor expended upon a raw
product, the further it is removed, as a rule,
from a general into a more special and narrow
field of demand.[1]

There is too often a vast disparity between
"real" and "nominal" assets.   The best machinery will not wear forever, and experience

---

[1] Growers' products, in fact, sell for cash all over the
world, except in New Zealand, where, according to our
consular reports, "articles of luxury," strangely enough,
command cash returns more readily than do the neces-
saries of life.

has shown that its worth is soon impaired, more or less, by new inventions. Soiled and unfashionable stock accumulates; goods held over depreciate; doubtful and worthless book-accounts multiply. Surely the statement of an upright man of business should reflect these facts. If he stands upon absolute verities, he will resolutely charge off such shrinkages, and place the value of his assets upon a real basis.

Where real estate figures in a statement, the mortgages and liens should properly be scheduled as liabilities, because they are a claim upon the general assets if the real estate does not satisfy them. In many statements the equity is merely shown as an asset.

Real estate is slow to be realized upon, and seldom brings schedule prices at forced sale. It is very likely to be blanketed with the heaviest possible mortgage before it reaches the assignee, and, under such circumstances, the value of the equity remaining is problematical.

It is complained that many houses, in irretrievable difficulties, have a propensity to hold on too long. Ethics would seem to require that, when a concern knows itself to be hopelessly insolvent, it should quit at once, and divide up, rather than keep on to multiply debts, filch a living, and end up with a lot of doubtful or iniquitous preferences. It was said of one such firm that, at last, its affairs were easily wound up, for its only remaining asset was a silver watch.

A statement sometimes shows a respectable capital which is nominally at the risk of the business, but which is really borrowed from relatives, with the secret understanding that they shall be preferred in case of disaster.

The balance carried in bank is good constructive evidence of financial strength, when it is not forced, like blossoms in winter, and bears due relation to other circumstances. But insolvency may lurk behind a big bank account, and knaves have too often flourished it as a decoy, for prudent business men to accept it in these days as a voucher of solvency and decisive gauge for credit.

We are not prone to do much exhaustive thinking, or be painfully anxious over the risks which others may assume; although it may be said that, as a rule, American business men cheerfully reflect their honest opinions, when reference is made to them in regard to the standing of an applicant for credit. And if two or three houses, known to be respectable and conservative, have acquired sufficient confidence in a man to give him a line of credit, and approve him to others, it is a fair presumption that he is, in some degree, worthy and responsible.

But such evidence is not always conclusive. A smart trader will see to it that those to whom he refers are qualified to speak favorably of, at least, their own specific experience with him. And it sometimes happens that houses thus referred to have been influenced to extend credit to the party in question solely by the example and reported experience of other houses, and that none have knowledge of his actual condition beyond that derived from rumor, or their own personal and limited dealings with him.

Again, it is conceivable that a trader may be heavily indebted to a house which knows him to be honest, but extended, and struggling along with an impaired, or limited capital; to weaken his credit would be fatal. Under such circumstance, a not over-scrupulous creditor might conceal the facts, and even help to fatten his debtor's assets against his probable bankruptcy. On the other hand, if he is a good and desirable customer, business jealousies and rivalries might prompt an artfully dubious report of him. Such cases especially manifest the value of the Mercantile Agencies, because, being wholly disinterested, their reports are made without prejudice or partiality.

Nor are instances lacking where the confident statements of a leading house have procured credit for a little-known dealer, whose subsequent failure exposed the fact that the concern which stood as his reference held judgment notes against him at the time they recommended him for credit; or, perhaps, a chattel mortgage upon his property, equivalent to a judgment execution and levy. It has been well said, that "the integrity of the many renders possible the fraud of the few."

The remark is often made, that concerns which cannot be trusted to "stand without hitching" always manage to obtain credit in some direction. The bait of a big profit is sure to allure some confiding dealer, and he who is regardless of how many cents he will, by and by, pay on the dollar can afford to be very generous in the small matter of prices.

Men of this stamp measure their strength by another's weakness, and are quick to see a vulnerable point. They bank largely on eagerness to sell. If the most desirable and salable goods "fly too high" for their pretensions, they become interested in the surplus stock of the last season, slightly unfashionable or shop-worn goods, "job lots," anything which, while having good value, it is especially desirable to be rid of. And they often inspire a degree of confidence in their intention to pay by artfully haggling over prices. It has been said, that the business of the world would be transacted by men possessing real means, if it were not anticipated by men without means.

The desire to sell goods is so general that the trade of responsible concerns is almost daily solicited, wherever in the country they may be located, and they will probably be offered all the credit they are entitled to, if they make known their condition. They need not beg for it. The receipt of an unsolicited order from a stranger

5

for the common sorts of merchandise is un-
usual.   If such order comes from a locality not
naturally tributary, it should be viewed with
increased caution, and only accepted when good
reasons are made apparent for wandering away
from customary and more convenient sources of
supply.

Yet the margin of profit on some articles is
such that the vender can lose every other bill and
still grow rich.   Sheet music, etchings, prints,
chromos, and other things, the chief cost of
which lies in the preparation of plates, or facilities for their multiplication at a trifling expense,
are examples.   So also are proprietary medicines
and similar articles.   It is evident that dealers
in such goods can afford to take greater risks
than those who sell metals, sheetings, or any
kind of staple commodities.   In fact, some
dealers in the former say they never refuse an
order, if they can learn that the party ordering
is actually in trade, and is not a fraud.

The type of buyers who inspire most confidence is frank, but not garrulous.   His claims
to credit are stated clearly, candidly, confidently, but in few words.   He meets no doubt until

the doubt arises. He identifies goods for his own conclusions, and buys, or rejects, upon his own judgment, and his "no" stands for a fact against all the arts of persuasion. He has a keen eye to price, but an equally clear and intelligent vision for quality and style, and he catches opportunity on the wing. The bearing of such a man proclaims that he is a living force, and implies that he at least deserves consideration.

If, in times of financial stringency, it became necessary for such a merchant to press his claims for discounts or favors upon his bank, he will set forth his needs frankly, and urge the equities of his case with dignity. He who cringes, and pleads for financial favors, or for credit, creates an unfavorable impression. It was Stephen Girard who said, to one that shed tears when asking for a loan: "The man who cries when he comes to borrow will cry when he is asked to pay." ·

The customer who can be overloaded with goods by a pushing salesman is a very questionable risk. If he is without experience, it is probable that, later on, he will acquire it at the ex-

pense of his creditors. If he is naturally credu-
lous, irresolute, and infirm of purposes, he is sure
to be a prey upon all sides, until he goes to the
wall.

Wise old Dr. Samuel Johnson made, many
years ago, a practical commentary on the modern practice of forcing goods upon a reluctant
customer. In urging the abolition of imprisonment for debt, he declared that failure to pay
was not always the crime of the debtor alone,
because the creditor shares the act, and often
more than shares the guilt of improper trust.
He invites, or urges, to the contraction of a
debt, in the hope of advantage to himself; and
proportions his profit to his own opinion of the
risk. And therefore, if the debtor is unable to
pay through misfortune, he should not be punished by the creditor, because both concurred
in the contract.

"Dating," means that goods sold, say in January, are to be delivered at once, but not invoiced
until March or April, when the specified term
of credit will begin. Purchasers insist that
they are justified in asking such credit conces-
sions, because of the exigencies of the season,

etc., and dating has, in some lines, become a prevalent custom. A large house in New York states that "dating" and "time stealing," or delay in payments due, cost it, on an average, more than its losses from bad debts, and many other houses estimate their loss of interest from this source as a serious item.

Some dealers think, or pretend to think, that if they pay interest on past-due bills and accounts, the creditor should be well satisfied, and make no complaint. But not so: the merchant is not a banker, and six per cent interest does not reimburse him. He needs his money to pay his own bills, and he needs it when it is due. Not to receive it is disappointing, and in violation of business equities. He is held strictly to the fulfilment of his own obligations, and he has the right to expect, and demand, that others shall keep their promise with him.[1]

---

[1] Suppose a trader owes half a dozen concerns, on account, $10,000, payable about January 1. He has in hand $5,000, November 1, but sees no way to get the other $5,000 until March 1. It is obvious, that if he pays half a book-debt two months before it is due, and the balance two months after it is due, he averages the

No merchant can reasonably expect to flourish long, in these days of driving competition, if he pays higher prices for his goods than his neighbor. But, as a rule, he is charged more for them, if he is careless and tardy in his payments, or if, from any cause, his credit is impaired or doubtful.

Lax business methods, or limited resources, multiplied into high prices for goods, sooner or later, give failure as a product. The old German proverb applies to mercantile affairs with increasing force: " *Lange Krankheit ist sichertodt.*" ("Long sickness is sure death.) And there are some who insist that, in this era of sharp competition, if a merchant cannot make his payments so as to secure cash discounts, the sooner he winds up, the better it will be for all concerned.

A Jewish merchant in New York, who for

---

payments. He should, therefore, promptly apply his $5,000 to his debts, *pro rata*. This may not be altogether as satisfactory to the merchant as regular payments on time, but few will complain, and it is better for all parties that the debtor should not wait until the last moment to pay his $5,000, and then plead for extended time on the remainder, with, or without, added interest.

more than forty years has maintained his credit, and grown rich in fair dealing, gives the following leaf from his experience: On a pleasure trip to the West, a few years ago, he read in a local paper that the head of a firm, which had a large credit account with him, had become involved with a woman in his employ, and that his wife had obtained a divorce on the usual statutory grounds. Without delay, he instructed his firm to close the account as soon as possible, and a few months later the Western firm failed disastrously.

A prominent merchant in Philadelphia relates the following: "One of the best men whom I ever knew, and who was in business for himself, called upon me one day to get me to accompany him to the noon-day prayer-meeting, at which he was a regular attendant. In answer to his solicitation, I said: 'No, sir; twelve o'clock to one o'clock is not my time to pray; it is my time to watch.' A few years afterward, he was doing business as an 'agent.' He had overlooked the divine injunction, 'Be diligent in business.'"

CHAPTER V.

IT is worth while to ascertain the nature of the patronage upon which a credit customer has to depend—whether upon farming, manufacturing, mining, or mixed pursuits; and what promise of success there is in the conditions which surround him. Perhaps he is attempting to conduct a first-class business in a poor neighborhood, or a business for poor people in a first-class neighborhood.

Agriculture is the basis of the national prosperity, and a farming community has always been considered stable and reliable. Yet, sections are subject to the possibility of drought, floods, or frosts, in unfavorable seasons, which destroy the crops. In such cases, the storekeeper may be unable to collect from his impoverished patrons, and become embarrassed, unless his resources are sufficient to tide him over to another harvest.

Agricultural conditions have changed essentially during the present generation. Farming is not as profitable as in former times, and, in some parts of the country, farm lands have declined in value, while the acreage under cultivation has also decreased, which is due to the fact that the lands could no longer be profitably cultivated.[1]

---

[1] The aggregate extent of this decrease, from 1880 to 1890, in a number of the older States, is shown by the Eleventh Census to be equal to the combined total area of several of the New England States. This census also shows that, in 1890, about 2,500,000, or rather more than half the farms, were under mortgage, the rate of interest paid being from 5.57 to 12.61 per cent. About 75 per cent of the indebtedness in the newer States appears to have been incurred for purchase-money, or for making improvements on the property.

More recent statistics indicate that the farms of the single State of Ohio, for instance, depreciated in value more than $50,000,000 during the year 1894, while the indebtedness of their owners increased about $8,000,-000. There were formerly but few renting farmers in the country, while now there are many, and they are increasing in number. In 1890, the percentage of the whole population inhabiting farms was 41 per cent; in 1894, 39 per cent. Since 1890, the rural population has increased but one-sixth as fast as the urban ; a portentous change to the wage-earner. In forty years rural or agricultural wealth has only quadrupled, while urban has multiplied sixteen-fold.

Hitherto, the natural fertility of our virgin soil, and the superiority of our farming implements, have enabled us to compete with other producing nations in the world's markets, even at a prodigiously greater cost for labor.[1]

But foreign competitors multiply, and adopt our labor-saving inventions, and farmers' prospects grow less hopeful. In addition to other prolific sources of supply, Argentina now makes claim to a vast area adapted to the growth of cereals, and her surplus of wheat last year was upward of a million and a half tons.

Prices of growers' products were never so low as of late; and it is probable, that if anything like "five-cent cotton, and fifty-cent wheat," are henceforth to be the rule, great numbers of our

---

[1] The Kansas State Board of Agriculture stated, two or three years ago, that the average cost of raising wheat in that region is $3.86 per acre, as against $5.07 in India, notwithstanding that the half-starved Ryot of the Gangetic plains gets but five or six cents a day for his work. This is equivalent to saying that the cost of raising a bushel of wheat in India is 53 cents, as against 30 cents in Minnesota, the Dakotas, or Kansas.

Professor Mulhall said recently: "An ordinary farmhand in the United States raises as much grain as three in England, four in France, five in Germany, or six in Austria."

farmers will abandon agriculture for more re-
munerative pursuits, and that still more farm
lands will lapse into wilderness.[1]
Manufacturing and mining communities, besides such vicissitudes as may arise from the
general laws of supply and demand, are sub-
jected to the possibility of labor troubles, which
may impair their prosperity. It follows, of
course, that when, in such a neighborhood, the
number of wage-earners is diminished, and earnings curtailed, the average resident trader must
share in the general distress.

---

[1] There has been a significant decline in the population
and prosperity of small towns during the last ten or
fifteen years. It is asserted that the States of Ohio,
Indiana, Illinois, and Iowa contain 6,291 townships, of
which one-half, or, to be exact, 3,144, declined in population between 1880 and 1890.

A South American correspondent of the New York
Herald wrote to that journal, in October of last year
(1894), as follows:

"If Argentine agriculturists desire to extend their
facilities for wheat-growing, they can do so to nearly
the same area, if not more, than in the United States.
Land that will serve for wheat-culture exists in nearly
all of the middle and southern provinces of the republic. There are at least 20,000 leagues of land, in the
hands of the general government, suitable for cereals,
while the area owned by private individuals is estimated to be at least 100,000 leagues."

The power of production is increasing in a much higher degree than the increase in the number of workmen employed, and it is probable that we have only seen the beginning of the complications which will accompany further industrial development.[1]

But while these facts are significant of startling possibilities for the more or less remote future, it is expected that they will affect existing conditions so gradually as to have little immediate practical importance from the viewpoint of the ordinary mercantile creditor.[2]

---

[1] In the 12th Annual Report of the Commissioner of Labor Statistics of the State of New York, made in February, 1895, it is asserted that "recent improvements in labor-saving machinery, especially in the printing trade, have caused a decrease in the number of employees from twenty per cent to sixty-six and two-thirds per cent; in other branches of industry, the decrease will average eighteen per cent, and in some instances it runs as high as sixty per cent." These figures are made up from returns furnished by labor organizations in the State.

[2] After a degree of density (of population) has been attained, sufficient to allow the principal benefits of combination of labor, all further increase tends in itself to mischief, so far as regards the average condition of the people. (J. S. Mill.)

It is not the poor, but those with vested interests, who now encourage immigration.

There is usually more cash afloat in a manufacturing town, and goods are sold more nearly
upon a cash basis, than in a purely farming
neighborhood, and collection facilities are better
in such localities.   Traders should, therefore, be
expected to collect more closely, and to pay with
promptness, and they may perhaps require less
capital to conduct their business successfully in
such towns.

A mixed-pursuit locality is less liable to extreme fluctuations of prosperity and adversity
than one which is "all cotton," "all wheat," or
"all corn," or its equivalent—a town chiefly de-
pendent on a single industry.   Paterson, with
its ninety or more silk factories, and twenty
thousand operatives, is an example of such a
place; so also is Fall River with its cotton factories, or Trenton with its numerous potteries.
These facts will suggest to careful merchants
the precaution of fire insurance companies,
which refuse to concentrate risks.

"Over-production" is held accountable for a
full share of the jarring competition, distress,
and failure among manufacturers and merchants
in recent years.   And, without doubt, there is

such a thing as over-production, relative to demand; but in no way can it be held in check
save by its own penalties. Men's desires are
boundless, and we shall more wisely try to stim-
ulate the world's consumption than attempt
arbitrarily to control production. To accom-
plish the former is the problem and quest of the
age.[1]

Natural law controls the development of
human affairs as surely as it regulates the seasons; and it is a suggestive fact that, under such
law, the wants of men increase as they become
civilized and enlightened. A demand arises for
the products of more advanced nations, and the
vitalizing energies of capital and credit multiply
with an expanding market.

---

[1] Two men came into a Broadway cable car. The
trousers of one were quite worn, and very ragged about
the knees, while the lamentably tattered condition of
the other man's trousers was only concealed when he
sat down. It would be interesting to develop the
opinions of these men in regard to the over-production
of trousers, for instance.

It was estimated, some years ago, that cloth was converted into clothing at the ratio of three parts materials
and two parts manufacturing and distributing, and
that the average annual consumption of clothing was
about $25 per head.

The temperate zone was first brought under subjection, in virtue of its more favorable climatic conditions and fewer physical impediments. The seeds of modern progress were not earlier planted in Arctic regions, because of the cold, nor in the Tropics, because of the heat. In torrid countries agriculture is hindered by dense forests; cleared land springs back into a jungle; harvests are destroyed by myriads of insects; the rivers are too wide to bridge; the heat enervates.

But now that civilization has subdued and appropriated the gentler zone—now that men have equipped themselves with labor-saving implements, and harnessed steam and electricity, enterprise is prepared to cope with the forces of nature in any part of the world, and it would seem that things are ripe for a general crusade of development.

Mediæval Mexico lies upon our borders. The great natural resources of the African continent and also of South America invite attention, and the surprising result of the war between China and Japan is significant of tremendous possibilities. Newly awakened Russian enter-

prise is already opening up vast regions with
incalculable resources, through the near completion of the trans-Asiatic railroad across
Siberia to the Pacific Ocean.

For many reasons, it is easy to believe that an
evolutionary, economic movement may at any
time arise, which, while largely absorbing the
surplus capital, will also give wider scope to the
surplus energies of the dominant races. One
effect of such a movement might be to lessen
the evils of so-called over-production, by extending the markets of the world, and stimulating
consumption of the products of civilization
among millions who are ignorant of them now.

But it is also possible that, when once the
teeming, imitative races of the East know and
prize these same manufactured products, they
themselves will soon learn to produce and return them upon the world in an ever-swelling
tide.

The current of affairs presents a different as-
pect from different posts of observation, and
there is usually a certain vantage-ground of
vision from which relations and consequences
stand out most clearly; like that famous picture

in Europe, which shows neither form nor design
but from one single standpoint. Some men and
things require to be seen near to be well judged
of; others are better observed at a distance.
Lookers-on at a game of chess often see broader
combinations than the players who are absorbed
in making the moves. There are men, with "no
admission except on business" written on their
foreheads, who are so occupied with petty details as to lose sight of the trend of their affairs.
They are like a man in a boat, who rows hard
and thinks he is getting on, while the man on
shore can see that the tide sweeps him steadily
backward.

Take an illustration from the wall-paper
trade. A few years ago, medium grades of this
article sold at three times their present prices.
Dealers who bought yearly, say $3,000 worth,
sold, and perhaps hung it upon the wall, at a
hundred per cent advance upon cost, and continued to do so as the price declined. They
had grown accustomed to this rate of profit. It
had been satisfactory, and they saw no reason
for alarm until, under some stress to meet obligations, they realized, perhaps for the first

6

time, that a hundred per cent yearly profit on $1,000 worth of goods was a different thing from the same ratio of profit on $3,000 worth. The store was as full of goods as ever, but they had only one-third of the former value, and expenses had diminished but little. The condition of the business had changed almost insensibly, and the result has been the failure of many small dealers, and some manufacturers and jobbers.[1]

It inspires confidence in the credit of a merchant, if he is known to regard business, not merely as a series of transactions, but as a matter of principles and methods. These are to

---

[1] A Broadway merchant of judgment and experience says he "sometimes recommends an easy-going customer to compute carefully the cost of transacting his business each day, each week, and each month; including, of course, all expenses, such as rent, clerk hire, light, fuel, etc. Add personal expenses, and place the totals on a card to be kept in sight, or within reach. Keep the sum of sales and profits day by day, and if expenses exceed profits in any month retrench in some direction." The same gentleman furnishes another piece of good advice for the trader. He says: "To hold your trade through hard times, keep up your assortment; don't let it run down. Buy little and often. Keep everything in sight, and nothing under the counter."

him what a compass is to the seaman, or a constitution to the State.   They give character and
stability to his dealings, and become a sort of
mental machinery, which balances the judgment,
and simplifies the solution of difficult questions.
Real business is neither a game of cunning nor
a dodging from one expedient to another, and its
vision extends beyond the next dollar.

Give two of the commoner sorts of men equal
facilities, and one will fail while the other grows
rich.   One is a good credit risk, and the other
is not.   Upon what different meat do they
feed?   Surely they must differ in essential characteristics; in judgment, prudence, honesty,
thrift, energy, economy, tact, diligence, etc.
Some men are like horses trained for speed
rather than endurance.   Your fussy man is
apt to be narrow, and to give his affairs much
attention, and little thought.   He has more zeal
than good sense.   He loses much labor for
lack of judgment to direct it.

The amiable, yielding man, who cannot say
"no," is often more applauded as a horn of plenty
by his customers than by his creditors, while the
resolute, pugnacious man may lack tact, and re-

pel or drive away business. One may have energy enough in his play, or at the call of passion, and yet lack the power of persevering work. "Some men would fail in Eldorado," said an American financier. As before stated, those who do not succeed can generally find in themselves the cause of their failure.

Most people believe more or less in "luck," and perhaps there is something in it, but the luck of your successful merchant is generally that of having faculties and using them. It is the luck of forecast, insight, and judgment, born in the sky, to be used with energy on earth. It has been said that lucky men are often more the creators than the creatures of circumstances.

A restless and progressive people like ours is prone to speculation, because it consorts with enterprise and growth; but ordinary business men, who have the reputation of being speculative, are not generally regarded as the best credit risks. Dreams of quickly acquired wealth, without industry, are apt to bear one away from simple integrities into very uncertain regions; and capital fights shy of "plungers."

Yet it is sometimes difficult to draw the line between speculation and commendable enterprise. Popular sentiment concerning a man's conduct of affairs is largely modified by his ultimate success or failure; and again, what at one time might properly be considered speculative and rashly hazardous may, at another, be really a prudent process of dealing. So may the undertaking of a wealthy man be entirely within the scope of his legitimate business, and yet a reckless, speculative venture for one with smaller resources.

It is to be noted, that speculations in one's own line of business seldom look as inviting to him as something outside, with which he is less familiar. It is the tailor who takes stock in a new pegging-machine for the shoemaker, and it is the latter who leaves his last to invest in a patent goose for the tailor.

Sharp men with schemes prefer to avoid those who are practically acquainted with the details of the project they seek to promote. There is no scope for the play of the imagination—not distance to lend enchantment.

In very many cases of failure, it is found that

the insolvent had become entangled in operations not necessarily connected with his regular business. "The lofty and sounding phrase of the manifesto" had seduced him into some specious undertaking, which has ended, so to speak, in a squirrel-track up a tree.

Farther down the list is the business man who is also an amateur gambler. It needs no gypsy to foretell his fortunes, whether he runs up against faro games, habitually bets on the races, or plays against Wall Street on margins.

If all these dollar traps were honestly conducted, and "luck" might be relied upon to break even, the money, in the long run, would surely go to the "kitty" in "percentages," "odds," or "commissions." It is the amateur, the "lamb," who "pays the freight."

Legitimate business implies mutual advantage through the interchange of equivalents; it is humanizing and beneficent. In gambling, mutual benefit is impossible. It is reckless, unthrifty, and demoralizing; and, once bitten by the gambling tarantula, the sufferer seldom learns wisdom from what he suffers.

A successful New York merchant discourses substantially as follows:

"I have no use for a man who gambles or gets drunk, and I will not sell him goods on credit if I know the fact. When I open a new account, I ask the debtor how far he wishes to go, and keep him to his limit, which I place against his account in the ledger. I want to know what kind of creditors he has to lean upon. If his capital is limited for the amount of his business, I prefer that he shall confine his purchases on credit to a few houses. It is for his own interest also, because, if he buys every-where, and gets behind in his collections and payments, some one of his creditors will be sure to jump down on him, and close him up. I don't want to do business for nothing, and when it is necessary to say 'no,' I do so boldly, but without unkindness.

"Those concerns which habitually, and upon the smallest pretence, make claims for allow-ance, or deduction, thinking they will be granted for fear of losing trade, I meet with manly re-sistance, rather than the 'mush of concession.' I make no such peace-offerings in business, un-

less justice requires it. I look upon them as
defeats, and they bring no thanks.

"There is a little in 'luck,' but the best credit
man is he who makes fewest losses and holds
trade. He should have good common-sense,
a knowledge of human nature, experience of
affairs, and be naturally cautious and conservative. I am superstitious about giving a
man credit after I have turned him down, unless there is a change in his circumstances.
Whenever I have been persuaded to do so, I have
lost by it. It is a good sign to see a man take
his sons into partnership. I am chary of a man
who does business in the name of his wife, nor
will I trust any concern, whatever its rating and
repute, if my instincts are against it."

Presentiments in regard to extending credit,
derived from so-called "instinct" or "intuition,"
are common among merchants and salesmen,
and such estimates are not necessarily independent of reason, or altogether unreliable.

Conclusions sometimes seem to leap into the
mind from nowhere, while the fact is that the
thinking faculty has reasoned them out without
realizing what it was about. They are the fruit

of an unconscious exercise of the intellect, which has been swiftly registering a multitude of perceptions, such, in our case, as the appearance and bearing of a man, his method of buying, the order and arrangement of his store, and numerous other conditions which surround him.

Moreover, it is a well-known fact that we are almost invariably attracted or repelled, in a greater or less degree, by the personality of a stranger, and we should sometimes be at a loss if compelled to express in words the reason for our impressions,[1] yet experience teaches that they are quite apt to be correct. Every face is either "a history or a prophecy," and we are reasonably justified, therefore, in paying heed, in the matter of estimating credit, to what we call our "intuitions."

Within recent years, the Jewish race has acquired a remarkable ascendancy in financial and commercial affairs in most of our trade centres; and it cannot be denied that their keen and active rivalry has developed, with some, a degree of prejudice, expressed often by invidious re-

---

[1] "I do not like you, Dr. Fell;
    The reason why, I cannot tell," etc.

marks concerning their characteristics and methods. But candid men will admit that their success is chiefly due to a natural genius for business, complemented by enterprise, self-confidence, and tireless energy.[1]

It is a brilliant race, with a strange history, and the annals of every art, and every science, are adorned with illustrious Jewish names. They have been less conspicuous as soldiers, inventors, manufacturers, and are seldom tillers of the soil; but statesmanship, philosophy, economics, jurisprudence, medicine, letters, music, finance, have all been enriched by their labors. Nor are they less distinguished in the field of philanthropy and practical charity.[2]

---

[1] The story is told of a Jewish new-comer in New York who, when asked how he, a stranger with small means, and speaking English indifferently, dared to plunge into competition with our two million people, made the characteristic reply : "But dose two million beeples must compete with me too, ain't it?"

[2] Those who have been led to believe that the Jews are generally harsh, unfeeling, and exacting employers are misinformed. A recent report of the United States Commissioner of Labor, giving statistics concerning the condition of working-women throughout the country, declares that female employees are treated with more kindness and consideration by Jewish employers than by any others.

Among our Jewish merchants are many who
are ideal business men; just, kind, sensible,
prudent, with a high sense of personal honor
and obligation, and alive to the value of an
untarnished credit. It will be admitted, also,
that there are some who are unpleasantly avar-
icious and selfish, crafty in dealing, "fresh"
and arrogant in prosperity. A considerable
proportion of our more recent Hebrew immigrants are ignorant and squalid, with characteristics as repulsive to their intelligent and enlightened congeners as to others.

Yet withal, the country could but ill spare its
enterprising and indomitable Jewish citizens;
and surely the time has come when no social or
commercial discrimination should confront them
as a class, on account of race or religion. It
is just and broadly politic that the credit of
every Jewish concern should, like that of any
other, stand upon its individual character, its
record, and its resources.[1]

---

[1] The Jewish house of the Rothschilds is probably the
most shining example of what financial genius can ac-
complish, when joined with integrity and favored by
fortune.

The house was founded by Mayer Anselm Bauer (born

It is remarkable, that countries differing widely in their social and economic conditions appear
to use credit relatively to the balance of their
trade. For example, Germany, Canada, and
Siam contrast strongly; yet it is believed that, in
each, ninety per cent of the business is done
upon credit.

American Consuls reporting from Belgium,
prosperous and progressive, and also from
China, at the time prosperous but stationary,
declare alike that eighty per cent of all transactions are based on credit. Somewhat vague

---

1743), who became a money-lender at the sign of the
"Red Shield," (Rothschild) in Frankfort. When, in
1806, the Elector of Hesse-Cassel had to flee before
Napoleon, he entrusted five millions in silver to Rothschild, who buried it in his garden for a time, and eight
years after repaid it with the most scrupulous fidelity.
This was the groundwork of his prosperity. Mayer
Anselm died in 1812, leaving five sons, who established
branches in the chief financial centres of Europe, the
brothers being equally interested. Nathan Mayer, who
died in 1836, has been regarded as the financial genius
of the family.

Various estimates have been made of the wealth of
this colossal house, which has been called "the seventh
great power of Europe," but they must be largely con-
jectural. It has, however, been prophesied, by men experienced in large financial matters, that, before the

consular estimates of the proportion of business done upon credit in France and Italy place it at sixty-five per cent of the total, while Holland leads the van as the most cash-paying nation in the world.

As there is probably no country where credit is extended so freely, so public sentiment is more lenient in the United States, in regard to business failures, than in other countries, and instances of complete recovery are more numerous here. The British trader is more conservative than the American; he neither gets rich, nor is ruined as quickly.

---

close of the next century, the Rothschilds will be worth five thousand million dollars. It has always been the policy of the Rothschilds to build up rather than tear down, wherein they differ from some of our American financiers; and in all the generations of the family not one member of it has brought a stain upon his character, either as regards his integrity or the purity of his life.

When the widow of Mayer Anselm was upward of ninety years old, a brilliant fête was given in her honor. She was quite deaf, and could not hear ordinary conversation, but she observed that those around her seemed anxious, and were talking earnestly. "What is it all about?" she inquired. "Bad news has come, and they are afraid we are going to have war," was the reply. "Oh, there won't be any war," said the old lady, "for my sons shan't give the kings any money."

Those among our retail traders who do a
"high-class" business give more credit than do
those who sell more cheaply to the masses.   The
middle classes pay best, and cash dealings become more general every year, yet the class of
easy buyers and bad payers does not seem to
diminish.[1] As a nation, we rest under the impu-
tation of giving little heed to economy.   With
the French, by way of contrast, the prevailing
idea in every household is that of economy; extravagance and excessive display being little
known out of Paris.

[1] Quoth Panurge to Pantagruel : " You ask me when I
will be out of debt.   The Lord forbid that I should be
out of debt.   Be still indebted to somebody or other, that
there may be somebody always to pray for you that the
giver of all good things may grant unto you a blessed,
long and prosperous life ; that will always speak good
of you in every company and ever and anon purchase
new creditors unto you, to the end that through their
means you may have a shift by borrowing from Peter to
pay Paul and with other folks' earth fill up his ditch.
It is a divine thing to lend ; to owe, an heroic virtue.
Yet doth it not lie in the power of every one to be a
debtor.   To acquire creditors is not at the disposal of
each man's arbitratement."

CHAPTER VI.

COLLECTION.

WHEN the executor of a certain eccentric physician's estate came to overhaul his books, he found, under numerous long-winded accounts, the words, "Paid by God," contracted sometimes into "Paid B. G." Being a pious man, he was much shocked; until he discovered that there were no corresponding entries in the cash-book, and that, instead of being used profanely, the words signified merely that the debt had been absolved, or wiped out, by the divine hand, in the death of the debtor. We seldom hear of a man who is willing to die to pay his debts, but there are many who are quite willing to live peacefully on and not pay. And it is this class which we come now to consider.

Next to being known as free and liberal in granting credits, nothing tends more to promote losses by bad debts, and to saddle undesirable customers upon a house, than the reputation of being lax and easy-going in collecting its dues. As a rule, that concern, whether it deals at wholesale or retail, which enforces prompt payments, is more respected, and loses little if any good trade by it.

There are of course times and cases when it is humane and expedient to show forbearance to a dilatory debtor; but the slipshod account which is perpetually in arrears, and can never be brought to a balance, merits little consideration, and is a good one to throw overboard. It is customers of this kind who avoid the patient and confiding house they owe, and sneak into rival establishments with their ready money, in order to obtain cash discounts upon their purchases.

A New York merchant insists that a concern may make more money, and prove a better credit risk in the long run, if its capital is scant, or barely sufficient, than if it be superabundant. And, he adds, that many who began rich, and are now poor, would now be rich if they had been poor at the start. His reason is, that the house which must have its money to meet engagements will be more active, will discriminate more cautiously in its credits, and will not permit overdue accounts to accumulate, which, like eggs, are apt to become addled with the lapse of time.

In historic times the debtor was at the mercy of his creditor. The ancient Romans cut the insolvent into pieces, and distributed them among his creditors; and, not so very long ago, the English clapped their helpless debtors into jail, and kept them there until they paid—or died. But the pendulum has swung, and, under the present condition of our laws, the creditor is practically at the mercy of his debtor.

The American people are, in many respects, prodigious sufferers from that uncertainty of the law which Burke called the "essence of tyranny." The nation is commercially one, but the relations of creditor and debtor, under the laws of the different States, vary essentially touching the rights and remedies of the one, and the duties and liabilities of the other; and they are, moreover, constantly changing.

The result is, that many times the too confiding or unwary creditor finds himself unex-

7

pectedly confronted with homestead, exemption, preferential, insolvent, or other sectional laws, which favor the debtor to such an extent as practically to frustrate all attempts at collection. So long as debts rest upon a legal basis, however slippery, uncertain, or inequitable that may be, there will be faithless debtors who recognize only their legal obligations. If the creditor appeals to the law, and such debtor can evade payment under the law, he will do so without scruple.

It has more than once been urged that laws for enforcing payment should be abolished, and that credit obligations should rest solely upon honor. Decent men everywhere regard their word of honor as inviolable, and a debt of honor as more binding than a legal claim.[1]

Probably such an innovation would quicken the public and private sense of honor and in-

---

[1] Charles Fox, the English statesman, an inveterate gambler, had long owed a onsiderable sum to a tradesman, who came upon him one day while he was counting a pile of money. "Now that you are so rich," said he, "you will surely take up your bill." "I can't," replied Fox, "this must all go to pay debts of honor." "And what is a debt of honor?" asked the creditor. "It

tegrity, and credit would more generally be founded on character. Public opinion would then brand the fraudulent or faithless debtor, and cast him out as unworthy of credit.

Many years ago, one of the most respected and prominent merchants of New York declared that, during the thirty most active years of his experience and observation, more money had been expended in lawsuits (if the value of time be included), than had been recovered by the aid of collection laws. He had sold merchandise upon credit to the value of many millions, aiming always to deal with those who esteemed

---

is an obligation which rests solely upon my word," said Fox. "Now," said the tradesman, tearing the bill to pieces, "mine is a debt of honor too." "Then I must pay it," said Fox, and he did.

Consul-General Strother, writing from Mexico, says the "proverbial Spanish sense of honor" prevails there in regard to debts. Credit is more freely given and less frequently abused, as a rule, than in more enterprising and speculative communities; and if there is bad faith in a failure, it is almost impossible for the bankrupt to recover his position.

Many instances of the effect of this sentiment can be found nearer home. For example: where States have enacted that debts for spirituous liquors should not be collectible at law, payments, as a rule, have been prompt and satisfactory.

character more than money, and making it the rule to credit none to a greater extent than he would had there been no law. His defaulted claims he had always collected, or compromised, without a suit.

But laws to enforce collections will never be rescinded so long as the innocent need protection from the guilty and designing. The matter is only referred to here in order to bring out more clearly the fact, that the majority of men pay their debts from quite other reasons than because they can be legally compelled.

The sense of moral obligation is even a stronger motive with great numbers of people than the sentiment of honor. Some unseen force makes the grass grow, and the stars shine, and whatever form of creed men hold, all feel that they are expected to do right, and generally admit that somehow, and somewhere, they must account to the Intelligence behind that force if they do wrong. They know also that false promises and broken engagements are not right.

There are other potent influences or springs of action, such, for instance, as policy, pride, or friendship, which move honest men to fulfil their obligations, when they are not provoked into obstinacy by reproaches and threats. All these facts lead up to the proposition that many tedious and expensive lawsuits and losses might have been avoided, had the fumbling creditor better understood the characteristics of his debtor, and wrought upon them with ingenuity and patience.

In cases of fraudulent default, the creditor's expedients are limited to out-manœuvering the juggling debtor by some swift master-stroke, such, perhaps, as recovering the goods by replevin, or to those legal proceedings which the circumstances warrant. Threats are sometimes, but not often, effective; the sharp knave regards them as the letting off of steam which is a sign that the vessel is not yet going to sea. If menace is used, that is most effective which lies in the firmness, not the irritation, of speech. When legal measures are once decided upon, they should be prompt and resolute.

It is the custom, with some concerns, to accept the first offer of a bankrupt in full discharge of his obligations, unless fraud is suspected, and, in many cases, this is certainly judicious

policy.   Legal measures involve the expense of
lawyers, tedious delays, the loss of time—and
perhaps temper—in attending trial, anxiety, and
the chances of final defeat.   If in the end successful, it is quite often found that acceptance
of the original offer would have been more
economical.

And again, it is easy to believe that a feeling
of relief may come to the broken trader, after
the shock is over which the announcement of
his failure has caused.   The crisis is past, anxiety over ways and means to meet maturing
obligations is at an end; he feels more cheer-
ful, and his mind naturally reacts toward a hopeful view of his position.   As yet, he has talked
chiefly with friends and sympathizers, and is
without a full foresight of the difficulties which
probably await him.   His first offer is, therefore,
likely to be his best.

Creditors are not necessarily harsh and per-
verse.   On the contrary, all are themselves
debtors, and the majority will probably express
sympathy, and give words of encouragement to
the unfortunate dealer.   But there are generally
some who must frown and scold, and the man

in difficulties is almost certain to encounter in-
difference and censure, and perhaps even im-
putations upon his integrity, whatever the circumstances of the case. Unexpected obstacles
and shrinkages confront him, promised remit-
tances are delayed, his business falls to pieces.
At length he becomes despondent, or exasper-
ated, and modifies his first offer.

A few mercantile houses have made it an inflexible rule—never to compromise with a delin-
quent debtor, but to reduce all overdue accounts
to judgments, and hold them for a hundred
cents on the dollar, with interest. This seems
a pitiless rule of action, to which no compas-
sionate creditor could long adhere, because it
does not discriminate in its treatment of an
honest, but unfortunate man, and a fraudulent
knave. Nor, aside from its inhumanity, does
the success of its results, so far as can be learned,
recommend it as a gainful course.

The concern which adopts this principle
toward its debtors may be known and avoided
by the fraudulent, but others also are deterred
from dealing with it. It becomes unpopular
with the trade. People have no liking for such

a house.   As it does not give, neither does it receive good-will.   The influence of the debtor and his friends is forever against it.   As a co-creditor, its selfish policy often retards or defeats the settlement which other creditors desire, and provokes them to resentment.   And, for all this, such a concern receives no compensation beyond the mere gratification of a vindictive feeling, because it appears to get no better returns in the end than the more lenient creditor.

There is hope of a debtor who has exceptional business ability, with character, youth, health, and energy, or of one who has expectations of inheritance, or wealthy relatives who will stand by him.   But chances of payment are too remote for a judgment against the ordinary bankrupt trader to be a very valuable asset, especially if he is heavily in debt.   If, however, he can manage to compromise with the larger creditors, he sometimes pays the smaller ones in full, in order to be able to use his name.

When John Doe finds, after his failure, that he can neither compound nor secure a legal discharge, he frequently continues on "under cover."   He puts up the name of his wife, or

perhaps a friend buys in the old stock and fix-
tures for him at a bargain, and he conducts the
business under the style of the "John Doe Company." He thus places himself out of the reach
of his creditors, and claims against him are
worthless. There is, to be sure, a chance that
he may prosper, and quietly buy them up after
a few years, as he can make terms. But, as a
rule, concerns do not prosper under borrowed
plumes; they find it almost impossible to regain
the confidence of the mercantile community and
a respectable credit, and have all they can do
to keep along without paying old debts.

Practical experience suggests that the creditor
should verify the statements of the defaulting
debtor, and possess himself of all the facts of
the case before he accepts offers of settlement.
"My estate is naught, it is naught," saith the
fraudulent bankrupt; but, after he hath settled
for a few cents on the dollar, he goeth his way,
boasting of the relative who will lend him
moneys to start afresh. It is not well for the
business world that such debtors get off too
easily.

It does not seem desirable, then, that a progressive merchant should apply any arbitrary rule of final action to all his insolvent debtors alike. Invariable harshness and obstinacy is neither just nor politic, while invariable leniency may pay a premium to fraud and incompetence. Circumstances vary in each case, and each should therefore stand upon its own special moral and legal equities and expediencies.

It is the principal creditors—the " pall bearers" —who are most interested to investigate the circumstances of a failure, and most anxious to reach the best and quickest results. Their action and recommendation, therefore, usually set the pace for the smaller creditors, if there be no suspicion that they are attempting to secure some advantage, whereby they can gobble up all the assets. In compromising claims, a quite common basis of settlement is 33⅓ per cent of the amount due.

Not infrequently, a large creditor keeps in the background, and as much as possible conceals his loss, lest it may damage his reputation and impair his credit. Many small creditors give their claims little or no attention, preferring to charge the account off, rather than expend time

and money in following it up. The sluggish in-
difference and inaction of small creditors is one
of the most perplexing obstacles in the way of
speedy settlement of a broken trader's affairs.
English bankrupt-law officials complain of this
same inertia, and it has also proved a retarding
factor under our own insolvent and bankrupt-
law proceedings.

The merchant, who has a claim for collection
at some distant point, takes a leap in the dark
if he entrusts it to a lawyer located there, without some certain knowledge of his character and
responsibility. Complaints are constantly made
of mismanagement and bad faith, in the conduct
of such cases, on the part of unprincipled attor-
neys, and also of their exorbitant charges.
Some of these gentlemen, learned in the law,
are prone to look upon the sum total of a claim
placed in their hands as all too small to bear
dividing, and they, therefore, calmly bolt the
whole of it, knowing that the far-away creditor is practically helpless.

The relations between the practising attorney
in a town, especially a small town, and the
party to be collected from, are often so friendly

as to prevent the former from pushing a claim vigorously which comes to him from a remote and unknown source. The lawyer's interests are largely local, and his expectations of support and advancement rest more upon the esteem and good-will of his townsmen and neighbors than upon the cold a pprobation of strangers whom he has never seen, and may never see or hear of again. It is only reasonable, therefore, to expect, that in many cases the interests of a friend and fellow-citizen will be favored and promoted, at the expense of a personally un- known client; and the experience of merchants bears out this expectation.

It is a better plan, if claims for collection are not given to one's own trusted attorney, to place them in the hands of a *responsible* Collection Agency. This generally involves no cost to the creditor, further than a small docket fee, unless the claim is collected, in which case ten per cent of the same is retained. Special terms are made upon large claims.

If legal proceedings are found necessary to compel payment, the creditor is required to ad- vance the sum which will be needed for disbursements in the suit, some portion or all of which may be returned to him, if it results successfully.

Some of the leading Mercantile Agencies take charge of the interests of creditors in cases of insolvency, and do also an extensive general collection business. They are especially qualified to perform such services advantageously, because of having active and experienced representatives at all points. These deputies, or sub-agents, obtain personal interviews, and often bring out facts and explanations which ward off lawsuits, restore harmony, and secure prompt payment. Like David Crockett's coon, the refractory debtor is willing to come down without waiting to be fired at.

CHAPTER VII.

CORPORATIONS.

A CORPORATION is created by the law, upon the general principle that the resources of many may, with advantage, be combined for certain specific purposes, under one flexible management.[1]

The advantages of a corporation over a partnership are that, while it may buy and sell, sue and be sued, and conduct its proper business like an individual, its shareholders are under no obligation to pay its debts. They are liable only to a certain extent, which varies according to the laws of the State from which its charter, or franchise, is derived. New York laws, for example, are considered as among the best for

---

[1] Chief Baron Manwood, an English jurist, was the author of the famous syllogism: "None can create souls but God: corporations are created by the King; therefore a corporation can have no soul." This is perhaps the reason why stock companies have so little sense of moral responsibility.

106

the creditor, and those of West Virginia as among the most "liberal," or poorest for the creditor.

The corporation idea is not new; it was put 'n practice by the ancient Romans, and, along down the centuries, corporations have superseded ordinary partnerships in commercial enterprises which were extra hazardous, or which required large capital. Chancellor Kent declared, in 1820, that the growth of joint stock companies in New York was "astonishing," and in 1821 the State tried in vain to check their formation.[1]

---

[1] The tendency to multiply corporations has, however, never been as great as just prior to the panic of 1893. The number of certificates of incorporation for the formation of stock corporations filed in the office of the Secretary of State at Albany, from January 1, 1893, to June 1, 1893, was 689. This is the largest number of stock corporations organized during any five months in the history of the office. During the corresponding period in 1892, only 479 were formed, the increase in 1893 being more than 44 per cent.

New York passed its first law for the taxation of corporate capital and earnings in 1880; this law was crude and unsatisfactory, and in 1885 it was amended. A very considerable revenue is now derived from this source, although it is claimed that the larger proportion of what is actually due still fails to reach the State treasury.

In 1844, joint stock companies, with a few exceptions, were for the first time, in England, enabled to incorporate under a general law, that is, without applying for a special charter.[1]   But members of these companies were still responsible for the debts to the whole extent of their fortunes.   In 1855, limited liability was introduced; but companies with this privilege must use the word "Limited" after their names.   It was said, in 1890, that one-third, at least, of English commerce was in the hands of incorporated companies.

Many corporations have been formed in this country for all sorts of purposes permitted by law, and in various fashions.   A common plan has, in times past, been substantially as follows: an inventor, for example, with his associates, organized a corporation, to which he transferred the rights to his invention, receiving as payment therefor *all the shares* of the company. The stock was, by this process, accounted "full-paid stock," and the holders were supposed to be

---

[1] The objects of certain companies, as for example, railways, involve an interference with private rights which requires special and direct charter, or authority, from the Government.

exempt from liability for debts of the company. The inventor's associates then bought from him a part of the stock at prices before agreed upon; the purchase-money, or a part of it, was placed in the "treasury" for a "working capital," and the company was ready for business. This was also a favorite method in working mining schemes. Thousands of companies organized after this fashion have lived and died—most of them have died.

But while, in the absence of statutory restrictions, a corporation may have power to receive payment, otherwise than in money, for a subscription to its capital stock, it has been held that stockholders are liable to creditors for the difference between the reasonable value of the property transferred and the par value of the stock.

The New York Statutes, of 1892, impose a liability upon stockholders "for every debt of the corporation, to an amount equal to the amount of the stock held by them respectively, until the whole amount of its capital stock, issued and outstanding at the time such debt was incurred, shall have been fully paid."

8

The members of an unincorporated company are liable individually for all its debts, no matter what agreement they make among themselves. But there is no personal liability attached to membership of churches, lodges, clubs, etc.

If persons organize under a general law for a purpose prohibited, or not authorized, by it, or if they fail to comply with its requirements in any material point, or if the statute under which incorporation is claimed be unconstitutional, the stockholders are liable as partners.

A more recent development is known as the "Industrial" corporation, which is based upon the grocery, brewery, or dry-goods store, etc. Among the reasons usually given for its formation are, that the proprietors are growing old, and they wish to place the business upon such footing that, while they remain interested advisers, they can be relieved of administrative labors and responsibilities, and, in the event of their death, the business may be continued without interruption or embarrassment. Or again, it is professedly done to give faithful and deserving employees an interest in the business. Some of these corporations are organized upon

a substantial and equitable basis, and are justly
entitled to confidence and credit.

But the industrial corporation too often re-
presents a worn-out plant, and a waning "good-
will," and the business, in a large proportion
of cases, is found to be capitalized largely in excess of its actual value. If earnings are all paid
out in dividends, as has been frequently the case,
the rich shareholder is reluctant to risk advancing from his private means for the benefit of
poorer ones when a pinch comes, and banks do
not, as a rule, take kindly to the paper of such
concerns without a good indorser.

A "trust" is formed by placing a majority of
the shares of each corporation which it embraces
in the control of persons called "trustees."
These agree to vote upon the stock so held for
the perpetuation of the trust during the time
agreed upon; to elect officers in each corporation
as provided for by law, and generally to direct
the business of all. Unity of purpose and action
is thus secured in the management of. vast and
widely distributed properties.[1]

---

[1] The Standard Oil Trust was organized in 1882, and
the Cotton Seed Oil Trust in 1884. There are now trusts

The "trust" was, three or four years ago, described as a "colossal, gigantic partnership, having no corporate function, owing no corporate allegiance, and capable of an elastic and irresponsible increase of capital stock. It may be a combination of corporations as well as of individuals, or firms, and its limits are boundless. It may embrace a hundred corporations, or any number more, chartered under the diverse laws of forty different States; with five hundred, or five thousand shareholders in each corporation, and each corporation may be chartered to carry on a certain business, different from either of the others. Trusts are now usually incorporated.[1]

---

in a great variety of articles, from cradles to whisky and coffins. It has been said that the American citizen has now to deal with trusts from the cradle to the grave.

[1] Trusts have, in some cases, succeeded in obtaining special State charters, granting certain advantages in the matter of taxation. The firms and corporations which combine to organize them turn over their property to the new corporation, receiving what they deem an equivalent in its stock.

If one of these great companies wishes to be listed at the Exchange, some promoters and stock operators are likely to be joined in the management, and its stock soon becomes a football of speculation. Sometimes the

Some of these great concerns may be "good" from the creditor's standpoint, but if their object be to monopolize business, by crushing out their competitors, they surely do not conduce to the "goodness" of others. An individual act, or circumstance, which is not important of itself, acquires strength, and may become illegal, when many combine to give it force. Union and concert invest it with effect against the public welfare.[1]

Those who oppose trusts aver that they are of the nature of conspiracies to enforce private interests, by combined action, regardless of the

practical men are gradually crowded out of the board to make room for more stock-jobbers. The original incorporators cannot recover control of their property, unless through a receiver. Profits shrink and expenses increase. Some of the assets are converted, in order to keep up the payment of dividends, and at length an issue of bonds is made. In short, the company is plundered, until, when the crash comes, little or nothing is left.

[1] Chief Justice Gibson, of Philadelphia, held in 1821, that "A combination is criminal whenever the act to be done has a necessary tendency to prejudice the public, or to oppress individuals, by subjecting them to the power of the confederates, and giving effect to the purposes of the latter, whether of extortion or of mischief."

rights of others. That they oppose honest and healthful competition, which seeks to merit success, with a ruthless rivalry, eager only to obtain it.[1] That they violate the spirit and menace the existence of republican institutions; are in restraint of trade, and against public policy.

President Cleveland said, in his last inaugural address: "The existence of immense aggregations of kindred enterprises, and combinations of business interests, formed for the purpose of limiting production and fixing prices, is inconsistent with the fair field which ought to be open to every independent activity. . . . They frequently constitute conspiracies against the interests of the people, and in all their phases they are unnatural and opposed to our American sense of fairness."

High State courts have, in recent years, repeatedly declared trusts illegal upon various grounds. Among other reasons it is held, that

---

[1] "A competitor strives to surpass by honest means; he cannot succeed so well by any other; a rival is not bound by any principle; he seeks to supplant by whatever means seem to promise success."—*Crabbe.*

the corporations which they embrace are vested by the chartering States with certain powers and privileges, on condition that they shall be used in subservience to the public welfare, and that their functions can neither be abdicated nor delegated.

The text of the Sherman Anti-Trust Law is as follows:

"AN ACT TO PROTECT TRADE AND COMMERCE AGAINST UNLAWFUL RESTRAINTS AND MONOPOLISTS.

"Be it enacted by the Senate and House of Representatives of the United States of America, in Congress assembled:

"SEC. I.   Every contract, combination in the form of trust, or otherwise, or conspiracy in restraint of trade or commerce among the several States, or with foreign nations, is hereby declared to be illegal.

"SEC. II.   Every person who shall monopolize, or attempt to monopolize, or combine, or conspire, with any other person, or persons, to monopolize any part of the trade or commerce among the several States, or with foreign nations, shall be deemed guilty of a misdemeanor, and, on conviction thereof, shall be punished by a fine not exceeding $5,000, or by imprisonment not exceeding one year, or by both said punishments, in the discretion of the court.

"Sec. III.   Every contract, combination in the form of trust or otherwise, or conspiracy in restraint of trade or commerce in any Territory of the United States, or the District of Columbia, is hereby declared illegal.

"Sec. IV.   The several Circuit Courts of the United States are hereby invested with jurisdiction to prevent and restrain violations of this act, AND IT SHALL BE THE DUTY OF THE SEVERAL DISTRICT-ATTORNEYS OF THE UNITED STATES, IN THEIR RESPECTIVE DISTRICTS, UNDER THE DIRECTION OF THE ATTORNEY-GENERAL, TO INSTITUTE PROCEEDINGS IN EQUITY TO PREVENT AND RESTRAIN SUCH VIOLATIONS.

" Approved July 2d, 1890." [1]

It has hitherto been found difficult to suppress trusts; they still flourish and multiply, defying public sentiment, and managing to evade legal restrictions.   Many fear that, as

---

[1] It is found that this enactment possesses very little restraining power.

they continue to increase, they will absolutely stifle competition in their respective fields, and, with the patronage and vast resources at their disposal, combine to influence such legislation as will give them a freer scope and a firmer seat in the saddle.

It is contended, on the other hand, that combination must in some way replace competition in the sphere of production; that great organizations are in keeping with the progressive spirit of the age; that numerous desirable results for the public benefit can only be achieved by uniting the resources of many, and that we have reached an era of development at which large consolidations of capital and ownerships are natural and necessary to social economics and advancement. It is also pointed out to us, that the free employment of organized association has favorably affected every social interest in American history, and that wherever there is most intelligence, and the best administration of affairs, there is the most corporate life and activity.

It will not be denied that there are many corporations honestly organized, and admirably conducted, which illustrate the best principles of corporate association, and show that they are beneficent when not perverted; but a wide-spread feeling or conviction also exists, that the arrogant and accumulating abuses of the corporate franchise should be rebuked, and suppressed.

In glancing over the legion of companies incorporated under our facile laws during the last twenty-five or thirty years, it may be noted that comparatively few of them have been capitalized at less than a hundred thousand dollars, and that a very large proportion have been based upon schemes of dreamers and swindlers, which have swallowed up all that has been put into them. Few have had an actual capital of the amount stated in their articles of incorporation, and it is unnecessary to say that the majority of them have utterly perished.

Special caution should be observed in extending credit to a company which puts forth its best ability to dispose of its stock;

To a company whose officers will make no detailed statement of its affairs;

To a company which gives notes, and has a large indebtedness to stockholders;

To a "parent" company, or a company being "promoted;"

To a "sub" company, on which the parent company holds a large portion of the stock, and exacts a royalty;

To an industrial company with a bonded indebtedness.

The creditor will remember that he contracts with the corporation, and not with its members, however high their standing and responsibility.

CHAPTER VIII.

THE MERCANTILE AGENCY SYSTEM.

SIXTY years ago, we had no railroads or telegraphs, and only a few small steamboats plying on inland waters. There was no ocean steam navigation, for it was not until 1838 that the *Sirius* and *Great Western* made their first regular passages, across the Atlantic. The great West was sparsely settled, and the total population of the United States was but 13,000,000.

It has since increased to about 70,000,000, or more than five-fold, while the volume of business has expanded several times five-fold. People then had fewer wants. They lived frugally, and produced for themselves many articles which are now made exclusively by machinery. There were fewer great fortunes, and less extreme poverty; and there was also less fraud and commercial knavery.

Yet, even in those ancient days, the lack of

any convenient method for investigating the character and responsibility of traders began to be seriously felt. Inquiries by letter were slow and unsatisfactory, and some of the larger houses employed travelling agents to visit their customers, and report upon their condition and home standing. But the information thus obtained was costly, exclusive, and temporary.

Many relied upon the references given them by those who applied for credit. But it sometimes happened that houses thus referred to looked with a jealous eye on the efforts of rival concerns to share the trade of good customers, or, on the other hand, might recommend the extension of credit to a doubtful debtor, in order to increase the probability of collecting their own claims against him. In any case, there was no certainty that the information thus received would be disinterested and truthful.

After the great financial troubles of 1837, which swept so many business men into bankruptcy, credits were much restricted, for merchants were all at sea in regard to the condition of traders throughout the country. But, with the slow reorganization of affairs, the need of some system for obtaining information became pressing, and, in 1841, " The Mercantile Agency" was put into operation in New York city.

It is said that the original nucleus was a book kept by the then prominent house of Tappan & Co., in which, for some years, had been registered all the information obtained respecting its customers. However this may be, both the brothers, Louis and Arthur Tappan, were identified with the organization in its early days.

The business of the agency was at first limited; but in 1846 Mr. Benjamin Douglass was admitted to a partnership with Louis Tappan, under the style of Tappan & Douglass, and he at once assumed the chief management and extended its operations. In 1854, Mr. Douglass succeeded to the business, and the style of B. Douglass & Co. was adopted, with the admission of Mr. Robert Graham Dun.

"The Mercantile Agency" now made rapid and substantial progress, and soon gained a recognized and assured position among the useful and necessary mercantile institutions of the country. In 1860 Mr. Douglass withdrew, and

ever since that time Mr. Dun's name has remained at the head of the agency.

A number of agencies, more or less extensive,
have been founded for furnishing reports since
" The Mercantile Agency" began its operations.
Many merchants will recollect those of W. A.
Cleveland & Co., Woodward & Dusenberry,
Potter & Gray, McKillop & Sprague, Bradstreet & Son, etc. The latter firm, founded
somewhere along in the fifties, was, a few years
ago, merged into " The Bradstreet Co.," which
is now a popular an l flourishing concern, with
many friends and a large number of subscribers. There are others whose reports are confined to a single line of trade, or are merely
local, and others still which furnish their
patrons with a list of persons, mostly lawyers,
in different localities, who answer inquiries by
letter.

European Commercial Agencies are conducted on a different plan, and the service they
render their home patrons would hardly satisfy
American merchants. The principal one in
Great Britain is probably that of Stubbs & Co.,
of London. There are also several on the Con-

tinent.   South of the equator a few small offices,
or bureaus, exist for obtaining and dispensing
commercial information, as, for example, the
"Prudencia," of Buenos Ayres.

It is the purpose of the writer merely to glance
briefly at the origin, operation, and economic
principles of a *system*.   If special reference is
made to "The Mercantile Agency" of R. G.
Dun & Co., it is because that was the pioneer
institution of the kind.   It has seemed fittest
for the purpose of illustration, and we will therefore follow its development.

"The Mercantile Agency" early discovered
that the demand for information was not confined to New York, but existed also in other
trade centres, in proportion to their extended
wholesale traffic.   And as the vast labor of reporting all the business men of the country could
not well be performed by a single office, or its
expense borne by the merchants of one city, a
system of auxiliary branch offices was gradually
extended to other points in the United States
and Canada, dealers at those places speedily becoming their patrons and supporters.

"The Mercantile Agency" has now upward

of one hundred and fifty branch offices, and it continues to establish them wherever the growth of business gives warrant of their usefulness.

Each of these branch offices has its special district, or field of operations, and its manager is responsible for the accuracy and completeness of the reports from that district.

There is a constant interchange of information between them, through the main office in New York. Each has also its subscribers, to whom it supplies the books of ratings, the weekly "Notification Sheets" of changes and events, and such special reports as may be required. It may also issue circular letters to its subscribers, without extra charge, which enable commercial travellers to obtain reports at any of its kindred offices in North America.

One might suppose that to be prepared to furnish instant and accurate information as to the character and responsibility of any and every business man on the continent, from Nova Scotia to the Pacific, or the remotest cross-roads of Texas, would furnish scope and swing enough for the most boundless energy. But not so, thought the proprietors of "The Mercantile

9

Agency." They have also extended their system of branch offices to the larger cities of Europe and Australia, and developed for their patrons reliable sources of information throughout the civilized world. They can furnish reports upon a Parsee banker of Bombay, a tea merchant of China, Formosa, or Japan, a spice dealer of Sumatra, or a trader of San Luis Potosi.

The representatives, or "reporters," who obtain most of the information for a first-class Mercantile Agency, are chosen with great care. They must be men of character, integrity, and experience; of good judgment and habits, free from prejudice, and naturally fitted for the duties they have to perform. These are often arduous, and always responsible; and they are apt to be pleasant or otherwise as the parties with whom they come in contact are intelligent or ignorant.

In the larger cities, a certain line of trade is generally assigned exclusively to the care of a "reporter" and his assistants. In time he becomes acquainted with every dealer in his line in his district. He knows the best-informed merchants and arbiters of credit in the larger houses, and exchanges information with them. He interviews bank presidents and cashiers, watches offices of record for transfers, mortgages, and judgments.

He acquaints himself with the abilities and characteristics of junior partners, managers, salesmen, and accountants, and has his own ideas of who among them is fitted, or fitting himself, to enter successfully into business on his own account. A new concern in his line catches his attention instantly; in fact, it is probable that he knows all about its affairs before its sign is up.

He enjoys the respect and friendship, and is often the confidential adviser, of many merchants in the line to which he is attached.

Reporters and correspondents throughout the country are selected with equal care, and with due regard to their freedom from prejudice and partiality, which might bias their reports. As a check upon them, or by way of verification, travelling agents are sent to the various districts, who make independent investigations. In cases where the reports are greatly at variance, or where they differ strikingly from former reports, the discrepancy is looked into by a third person. The reports of a first-class agency should, of course, be truthful and explicit; they must also be frequently revised, and, last, but not least, promptly furnished.

The excellence of an agency depends also largely on the universality of its reports. If it can furnish information on but one-half, or two-thirds, of the traders in a certain line, its value to a general dealer in that line is obviously limited. As it is, in fact, entrusted with the business of others, the nature of its service is that of a deputy or susbtitute, and the relations existing between it and its subscribers are closer than those between buyer and seller. They are largely mutual, and, in proportion as its hands are strengthened by its patrons, it can do more and better work for them. The greater their number, and the higher the compensation received, the more it can extend and improve the quality of its information for the benefit of all.

Justice has been defined as the virtue which consists in giving every one his due; and the steady and substantial growth of " The Mercan-

tile Agency" for fifty years bears witness that
this must have been the cardinal principle of its
proprietors.   It has also demonstrated to the
public that, for the object in view, no more satisfactory system has been, or perhaps can be de-
· vised, than that by which its operations are conducted.   It has no motive to injure or misrepre-
sent any one.   On the contrary, the best interests of an agency prompt it to get as near the
truth as possible in every report, because the confidence of those upon whom its prosperity depends will surely be proportioned to the accuracy of its information.

Objection has sometimes been made that the
system tends to create a sort of moneyed rank,
or that it practically discriminates against men
of small means, and in favor of the rich.   But
this is not true.   A respectable mercantile
agency refuses to become the arbiter or censor of
any man's affairs.   It simply records what it
can find and verify.   It deals in facts, rather
than opinions; yet in its ratings and reports,
reputation and character must be as carefully
considered as mere ability to pay.   And,
furthermore, if wealth confers any distinction,

it is not in this country hereditary, and is accessible to all. Death brings division of property, and new financiers come to the front.

Nor does the agency make public its written or printed information. It is communicated only to annual subscribers, specifically for use in their own business, "as an aid in determining the propriety of giving credit," under the written pledge that it "shall be strictly confidential, and under no circumstances be communicated to others."

No intelligent man can expect another to entrust him with his property without inquiry to ascertain if he is worthy of such confidence. If he is honest and responsible, he cheerfully invites it. If he objects to it, it is a reasonable inference that the result would be unfavorable to himself.

He who asks for credit virtually challenges such investigation, and accords the seller the right to make it. Nor can this right be confined merely to the seller personally. *Qui facit per alium facit per se;* he may deputize his salesman, or his bookkeeper, or he may properly confide the troublesome and delicate service to an organization which will perform it for him promptly, and at the least expense to himself.

Probably the greatest usefulness of the mercantile-agency system consists in the protection it gives against incompetence and dishonesty. It traces absconding debtors wherever they may locate, exposes false and fraudulent representations, and gives caution against the doubtful.

If, for example, a trader in New York premeditates a fraudulent failure, he stretches his credit limit with his accustomed houses, and strives, right and left, to open new accounts. Requests for reports at once pour in upon the leading agencies, and an extraordinary number of inquiries concerning any person, or firm, signifies either distrust, or exceptional conditions of some kind, which call for prompt investigation.

But the mercantile agency does far more than this. It places in the merchant's or manufacturer's hands a complete list of the solvent buyers of the country, states their resources, gives their home reputation for ability, thrift, and integrity, and the promptness with which they meet their obligations, from the actual experience of those from whom they buy. It is constantly on the alert to discover and apprise its patrons of changes which may affect their interests, and it prevents delay in the shipment of goods to any part of the country if the purchasers are responsible.

The agency system is of vast benefit also to buyers in all parts of the land, for it expands far more than it restricts credit. It opens the entire markets of the country to every substantial and upright dealer, without regard to the locality of his business. The books and records of the agency are his best letters of introduction. He need not now, as formerly, be confined in his purchases to a few houses where he is personally known. It tends also to protect him from the injurious competition of irresponsible and unprincipled traders, and in many other respects renders him essential service.

Feeling that he and his affairs are observed and open to the scrutiny of the business world, the country merchant may naturally become more prudent and conservative in his dealings. It tends to check extravagance, restrains him from doubtful speculation, and promotes in him a finer sense of the value of industry, and thrift, and of character, for he knows that the agency mirror will reflect what he is. If he finds that his credit suffers from his uncertain habits, his lack of economy, or of punctuality, he is driven to retrieve himself, and, like the wounded oyster, "mend his shell with pearl."

The American mercantile agency system is unique; nothing comparable to it exists elsewhere, but it is a natural outgrowth of our peculiar needs and conditions. The great extent of the Republic; its subdivision into numerous sovereign States with diverse laws; the freedom of interstate traffic; the rapid growth of the country; the energy and enterprise of the American people; their cosmopolitan and somewhat migratory characteristics; the general use of credit, and the absence of that governmental scrutiny of individuals which exists in many European countries,—all combine here to render the institution indispensable.

The mercantile agency of the future will probably be conducted upon substantially the same methods as at present, unless essential changes occur in commercial conditions, which cannot now be foreseen.   It is, in fact, difficult to conceive of any general plan for gathering and distributing the required information, which could be substituted with advantage for the one now operative.   But it is believed that the institution is progressive, and that it will continue to multiply checks on fraud, and in other respects further promote the interests of the mercantile community.

Commerce goes hand in hand with intelligence.   It pays the wages of science, and is the patron of art.   It is fruitful of ideas, of systems, of railways, ships, telegraphs, cities, machines, manufactories, fabrics, houses, comforts, and conveniences.   It is the nation's life-blood in circulation.   Who shall deny it the right to claim all facilities for the extension and security of its operations?   Commerce required the mercantile agency system for its protection—and it was created.   It has grown with the growth of the country, and so long as the credit system exists it will remain, for confidence is the foundation of credit, and knowledge is the cradle of confidence.

It has now become interwoven with the trade

of the country, and is so generally leaned upon, that were it to be, from any cause, suddenly abolished, or its operations seriously curtailed, uncertainty, confusion, and distrust would come at once. Credits would shrink, and the distribution of merchandise be restricted.

CHAPTER IX.

A NOVEL and interesting system for indemnifying business men against excess losses from bad debts was put into practical operation, about six years ago, by the United States Credit System Company, whose headquarters were in Newark, N. J. Since then, several organizations, conducted substantially upon the same plan, have entered the field as Credit Indemnity or Guarantee Companies, some of which are still in active operation.

Broadly stated, the principle upon which this system is based is, that in each line of business there is a certain specific average of losses on credit sales. Up to this point, the insuring merchant or manufacturer must himself take the risk; but he may obtain a certificate of insurance against further losses, within certain limits, by paying something like three or four per cent premium on whatever amount is covered by his certificate. He is, however, restrained from taking reckless risks, by the ratings and reports of the leading mercantile agencies, certain low grades of credits being. exempted in the guarantee.

The premium exacted has usually been a fixed one, in proportion to the amount of insurance, the varying quantity being the stipulated percentage of loss which the insured must bear before his indemnity begins. This changes with the nature and extent of the business, it being higher for a small than a large concern.

It is claimed that, while careful provision is made against fraud, there is no irksome espionage upon the insured, nor is any meddlesome supervision or interference with their business necessary. The company is to be notified at once of excess losses, and upon due proof of the same they will be adjusted, and paid within a reasonable time.

The new and ingenious feature of the plan lies in the fact that the interests of both parties jog on together until the insured reaches the stated limit of "average losses." To this point, the less the loss, the better for the merchant, and the farther off the insurer's risks. If not reached, the premium is all profit to the insuring company, while the merchant has had the satisfaction of feeling protected against disastrous mercantile contingencies, as his insurance policy has protected him from loss by a possible fire.

A company for guaranteeing credits, which operated on a seemingly more speculative and hazardous plan, was also organized in New York several years ago. This was simply to guarantee the payment of notes and accounts, on such terms as might be agreed upon in each case. But its offerings were chiefly doubtful or rejected risks, and but few which could be deemed reasonably safe. This company was unsuccessful, and soon withdrew from the business.

There should be no more difficulty in ascertaining the average losses in each kind of business, through an extended series of years, than there has been in acquiring a knowledge of the averages upon which all fire, marine, life, and accident insurance is based. And it would surely seem that, if equipped with the necessary data, a well-ballasted company might as safely, as profitably, and as equitably, insure against credit losses as against losses by fire or ship-wreck. But there are some notable differences and perplexities to be considered.

A necessary condition for the success and permanence of any insurance company is that the premium paid for insurance shall be remun-erative. It is from the premiums that the losses must be paid, or the business will soon perish. Fire, life, and marine insurance have generally proved profitable to their respective companies in all parts of the world. Losses in most kinds of insurance vary so little from year to year, that an adequate premium for an ensuing year might, with a watchful regard to current changes, be fairly predicated upon the experi-ence of several preceding years.

Yet fire insurance, for example, is now so care-fully administered that the data, from which to establish the general premium rates, is not taken merely from the experience of any one company, but from the accumulated and combined experi-ence of all. Still, even these rates constantly fluctuate. It will be observed, that if a season's fires have been large and numerous, and losses unusually heavy, premiums are advanced all along the line.

But credit insurance is subject to greater and more frequent vicissitudes. The movement of mercantile affairs in uncertain cycles of elevation and depression depends upon many circumstances, which can neither be foreseen, nor guarded against, by the credit insurer. Panics seldom come on schedule time, but often suddenly, and when least expected; and the losses of a Credit Indemnity Company, in a year of panic and liquidation, may easily exceed the losses and sweep away the profits of several ordinary years.

It is evident, therefore, that the premium demanded by such a company must be such as will cover varying degrees of mercantile prosperity. It must be large enough for the company to gain a reserve when trade prospers and losses are few, so that it may be in a position to meet the exigencies of a crisis which is liable to come at any time, and may not come for years. On the other hand, it must not be much above the actual risk incurred by prudent and intelligent merchants, or they will decline to insure.

The business of insuring credits could not be profitable in calamitous times, if the premium were based on *average* losses. A company insuring credits upon this basis, during a season of panic, could only hope to find compensation for extraordinary losses through a continuation of business, at the same premium rate, when prosperity returns.

But people insure against fire and wreck because such casualties are so largely due to fortuitous circumstances, which no ordinary exercise of wisdom can foresee or prevent. The credit losses of a mercantile concern depend less upon mere chance, and it has often been proved possible for experience, skill, and prudence to limit them to a very low figure. It therefore remains to be seen, whether the better class of merchants will continue to insure their credits freely, at a long-range premium, when trade thrives again, and losses are small.

It is thus manifest that it can be no easy matter to determine upon an inflexible premium beforehand, which will be reasonably safe for

10

the insuring company, and satisfactory to the insured; because the rate must come first, and a wide range of uncertainties in either direction afterward.   The cost cannot be known, until the goods are sold.

Yet withal, reasons are as plenty as Falstaff's blackberries, why a company, which can furnish absolutely safe and equitable insurance against credit losses, should receive welcome and support, and become, in time, a bulwark of trade. If such possibilities do not lie within the scope of the system at present operative, or in some modification of it, it is reasonable to think that some other plan may in time be devised, which will extend this valuable privilege to the business community.

The companies which have been organized for this purpose have shown commendable enterprise, but they have been unfortunate in stumbling upon hard and unfavorable conditions so early in their career.   Yet the large number of substantial concerns, in all parts of the country, which have been and perhaps are still their patrons, shows a willingness to sustain them, and manifests the general desire for some form of protection against credit losses.

There are many reasons to believe that Credit Insurance will receive a full measure of public confidence and support when, and only when, it has passed through its experimental stages, and settled its foundations firmly upon broad, accurate, prudent, and approved generalizations. The great, trusted and successful company of the future will be a growth or an evolution.

CHAPTER X.

A UNIFORM BANKRUPT LAW.

IT is a constant source of perplexity and loss to American merchants, who give credit, that while all the people speak the same language, use the same kind of money, obey the same national control, and trade freely throughout the general domain, each State has its own special laws for regulating the property rights and duties of its citizens.

Forty or fifty independent legislation-mills in the country grind out, every winter, from five to eight thousand laws, many of which are incongruous, unjust, or oppressive; and there is a constant ebb and flow of enactment and repeal, bewildering even to a Philadelphia lawyer. Worse still: lobbyists swarm at every State capitol, and statutes are made to order for rich men's money, or the votes of the rabble. Surely, no nation on earth has greater need for a uniform system of bankruptcy than the United States.

The Constitution vests in the general Government the power of making such a law, while it forbids the States to impair the obligation of contracts. And although, in the absence of a National law, some of the States have enacted insolvent laws, such statutes are incomplete and unsatisfactory.

The foundation doctrine of an insolvent law is, that it extends only to exempt a debtor from liability to arrest or imprisonment for debts previously contracted, on condition of his giving up all his property for the benefit of his creditors; that of a bankrupt law, to protect his future acquisitions from his creditors.

Insolvent laws are therefore passed for the benefit of debtors, and they bind only citizens of the State which enacts them. Under none of them can a debtor secure a release from non-resident creditors: few provide for even a limited discharge, except through the clemency of creditors, and they afford the latter but scant protection against fraud and chicanery. All State laws on the subject are suspended when a general law of bankruptcy is in force, and the failure of Congress, for many years, to pass such a law is thought to have been unfavorable to the best interests of the country.

Congress passed the first bankruptcy bill in the year 1800, and repealed it in 1803. Another was enacted in 1841, and repealed in 1843. Both were passed for the relief of debtors who had failed during the preceding commercial crises. The loose and burdensome measure of 1867 was amended in 1874, and repealed in 1878.[1]

Early in the century, the eminent Chancellor Kent, and other lawyers, were of the opinion that a law which discharged debts without full payment was demoralizing. It was thought to encourage reckless trading, speculation, and ex-

---

[1] This law of 1867 was framed by Congressman Jenckes of Rhode Island. It was an attempt to secure equity by forbidding preferences, and by dissolving all recent attachments upon the debtor's property; and to relieve honest debtors by granting them discharges on certain conditions. The amendment in 1874 rendered it difficult and expensive to force a debtor into bankruptcy. It also enabled him more easily to obtain a discharge by composition, which was objected to as giving too much power to the debtor, and too little to the courts.

travagance, and as tending to diminish that
wholesome horror of bankruptcy which all men
should feel.

But experience, under the vastly changed conditions of more recent times, teaches otherwise.
Officials familiar with the administration of the
present English bankrupt law declare that it
tends to promote more prudent habits and
greater carefulness, that its operation gives
much satisfaction, and shows a steady and per-
manent improvement.

It is now generally conceded that the material
advantages of a well-devised bankrupt law far
outweigh all objections that can be brought
against it, and that it is also desirable on the
ground of common humanity.

During the progress of the century, legal
severities toward the unfortunate have been
more and more relaxed or mitigated. Judge
Story early called imprisonment for debt a measure "disgraceful even to an enlightened despot-
ism," and it is now, happily, a thing of the past.
But that profound and accomplished jurist also
declared that he could recognize no distinction
between the injustice of imprisoning the body

of an honest debtor, and of monopolizing all his future earnings.

The law formerly regarded the bankrupt as a *quasi* criminal. It now generally looks upon him as neither innocent nor guilty, but as one whose conduct requires examination. If it be found that his failure is the result of honest misfortune, the law, under every civilized flag but our own, distributes his property among his creditors, and compassionately grants him a discharge; but denies it to his faults.

If any think a well-planned bankrupt law to be merely a legislative act which enables a lot of debtors to escape their obligations, they mistake its scope and spirit. It operates also to frustrate and punish fraud, and protect creditors. It bears the same relation to estates in liquidation, because of dishonesty or failure, that probate laws bear to the estates of deceased persons.

Without doubt, the abuses practised under the administration of each of the former bankrupt laws gave much cause for dissatisfaction; and there are some who profess to believe it impossible to pass a wise law, because the old ones were defective. But this is to deny that experience and intellectual progress can bear fruit.

Our early legislators had, upon this subject, but a narrow range of precedent and practical knowledge from which to draw conclusions. The nation has since observed and cogitated, and now thinks itself qualified to frame a single law, which shall avoid the errors and embody the wisdom of all the many State and National insolvent and bankruptcy laws which have preceded it.

That such a measure has, in fact, been already prepared, those familiar with the provisions of the Torrey Bill firmly believe. Every part of this bill has been long and carefully scrutinized, both by legal knowledge and mercantile experience. It has been much amended and improved from the original draft, and is now considered ripe for enactment.

Congressional committees have warmly approved the Torrey Bankruptcy Bill, and urged its passage. In response to the popular, non-partisan and non-sectional demand, it will probably soon become a law.

In June, 1892, Mr. Oates, chairman of the

House Committee on the Judiciary, submitted a report on the Torrey Bill, which characterized it as follows:

"A summary of the bill in five words: A square deal all around."

"A summary in a paragraph: a measure for the discharge of honest insolvents, the diminution of fraud, the prompt and economical administration of bankruptcy estates, the maintenance of integrity in transactions on credit, and the promotion of commerce."

Many commercial bodies have addressed Congress in advocacy of the Torrey Bill. Among them is the National Board of Trade, which, at its session in Louisville a few years ago, adopted a memorial to Congress, commending its provisions, and requesting its passage. This memorial declared that, in the opinion of the Board, the Bill, if made a law, would effect the following results, viz:—

1st. Diminish the number of failures.

2d. Increase the amounts paid by insolvent estates.

3d. Abate the class of fraudulent adventurers.

4th. Hold in check that class who make a business of failing.

5th. Put an end to the system of legalized robbery, constantly perpetrated through concealed or pocket judgments founded in fraud.

6th. Substitute one uniform, equitable law for the numerous incongruous and inefficient State insolvency laws.

7th. Provide a uniform collection law.

8th. Restrain compulsory processes against honest, solvent, but embarrassed merchants, who, under present conditions, are liable to suffer from contests between creditors to secure preferences.

9th. Repress commercial wrongs not now designated as crimes, but forbidden in the Torrey Bill.

10th. In effect increase the invested capital of all dealers by giving more general confidence.

11th. Secure to honest unfortunates a discharge from the excess of their indebtedness over the amount of their assets.

12th. Check the fraudulent system of individual creditors obtaining from bankrupt debtors a larger percentage than others receive, as a condition precedent to discharge.

13th. Prevent fraudulent preferences.

14th. Secure a prompt adjustment of matters in controversy, by arbitration, compromise, or litigation.

15th. Provide for holding creditors' meetings at places which will best serve the convenience of the greatest number.

16th. Secure an equitable division of the assets of insolvents among their creditors, quickly, and at a minimum cost.

If Congress will enact this or a similar bill, and its operation fairly justifies the claims made in its behalf, it will prove a benefaction to the commercial world. The wonder will then be that, for seventeen years, we have tolerated the inequitable, confused, exasperating, and unnecessary conditions which have prevailed in the absence of such a law.

CHAPTER XI.

PANICS.

THE people have repeatedly suffered during the century from visitations of what, for want of a more definite word, is loosely termed a "panic." From the fact that these calamities have never been produced by natural causes, such as earthquakes, pestilence, or famine, they have sometimes been held to signify some radical defect in our economic system, which can only be remedied by reconstructing it upon a different basis.[1]

The English economist, W. Stanley Jevons,

---

[1] A writer in the English *Journal of the Statistical Society* states, that in the 11th, 12th, and 13th centuries, the average was, in England, one famine every fourteen years. Authorities like Godwin, Ricardo, and Mill say, that we have succeeded in rendering a famine "next to impossible." The masses no longer fear a famine, but its opposite, a *glut* of those commodities which they themselves produce and most need, because such a condition is followed by distress among them.

related panics to the sun-spots which, in modi-
fying the rainfall, affect crops and prices.[1]
Others refer them to over-production. John
Stuart Mill pronounces this an error, and says
panics are caused by a contraction of credit, and
the remedy is a restoration of confidence. This
seems about like saying that sickness is due to
ill-health, and the remedy is to get well. A
panic, and a general loss of confidence, are
practically equivalent and reciprocal terms.
One is as much the cause as the effect of
the other, and either produces contraction of
credit.

England has had, since 1814, as many panics
as we; and so has France, except that she escaped that of 1873, because of the Franco-Prus-
sian War. Sometimes the panic has appeared
a year or two earlier or later in one country

---

[1] In a recent issue of *Les Sciences Populaires*, Professor
Mascari assigns the latest maximum of sun-spots to
August, 1893. The last sun-spot maximum preceding
this occurred early in 1884. This record is made up
by the Professor chiefly from his own observations at
the observatory of Catania. It may interest some to note
the coincidence, that both 1884 and 1893 were years of
panic.

than in the others, but its effects have been practically simultaneous in the three, and to a
greater or less extent throughout the commercial world.

We have been accustomed to think that, while
the changing phases of foreign affairs—the
financial attitude of other nations, and their demand for our products, might bear close relation
to our welfare, they did not cause our panics.
These have nearly always been popularly and
perhaps plausibly attributed to domestic events,
such as unwise legislation, tariff changes, scant
crops, credit inflation, or unsound currency.

But, unless the above facts are no more than
coincidences, they would seem to indicate that
these sweeping commercial revulsions really
originate from causes common to all the panic-
stricken nations, and that our national occur-
rences are but proximate or secondary causes.
Perhaps some philosopher will arise and tell us
that a recondite tendency to panics is to be
found in modern civilization, or, deeper still, in
the natural foibles of human nature, to be
developed, like great epidemics, by some unknown influence.

It is not difficult to see now, why we have been afflicted with a full share of the world's panics. The amazing progress of the country, and the nature of its institutions, have seemed to render it necessary to attempt the solution of many pressing legislative and economic problems in an experimental way. We have, therefore, lived, more than the people of any other great nation, in a constant state of uncertainty —not perhaps as to general results, but in respect as to what to-morrow's legislative measures may have in store for us as manufacturers and merchants.

Trade has its natural laws, under which its highways, methods, and usages are established along the line of least resistance. But they must be constantly readapted to changing conditions; and constant change, or apprehension of change, creates that uncertainty of the future which renders business speculative, hazardous, and demoralizing. Mercantile interests generally, and the credit system especially, demand a stable basis upon which to calculate. Business men prefer to anchor upon even tolerable conditions, rather than drift in shifting channels, which is always dangerous.

The panic of 1814 followed the war with England in 1812. The blockade of our ports had prevented the export of produce, and drained away our specie. Peace came in 1814, when England inundated us with her wares and drove our own manufacturers and merchants out of business. The war debt created exceeded $80,-000,000. Much paper money was afloat, and the want of a solvent currency was severely felt. The banks, except in New England, suspended specie payments.

In 1816, Congress chartered, for twenty years, a National Bank, with a capital of $35,000,000. It was located at Philadelphia, but permission was granted to establish branches elsewhere, under certain conditions. There were twenty-five directors, five of whom were to be chosen by the President, and all were made personally liable for violations of the charter. A vast issue of paper money followed. In 1818, the bank had passed the safety line, and was at the mercy of its creditors. A panic was pre-
11

cipitated upon the country, and there was much distress.[1]

Liquidation ceased in 1819 and prosperity returned. But we had not learned how to deal with banking institutions, and "wildcat" banks of issue sprang up in various parts of the country, because they could be organized with little or no tangible capital, and were subject to no

---

[1] Our patriotic forbears seem to have been as much befogged on the money question as are some of our fellow-citizens. Here are some specimen views:

"Do you think," said a delegate to Congress during the Revolutionary War, "that I will consent to load my constituents with taxes, when we can send to our printer and get a whole wagon-load of money, one quire of which will pay for the whole?"

An address issued by Congress to the States, in 1779, contains these words:

"Let it be remembered that paper money is the only kind of money which cannot take unto itself wings and fly away. It remains with us; it will not forsake us. It is always ready and at hand for the purposes of commerce, or taxes, and every industrious man can find it." At this time Congress had no power to tax, and efforts were made to keep the paper currency from sinking in value by legally regulating the prices of commodities.

Prior to these events, Adam Smith, author of the famous "Wealth of Nations," had compared the use of gold and silver money to a highway on the ground; that of paper money to a wagon-way through the air.

effective supervision or control. There was, for several years, an abundance of currency; but a crisis came in 1825, and again confusion and distress prevailed, although England suffered still more severely.[1]

After recovery, business continued active and money plentiful until, in 1831, there were some considerable embarrassments, due to expanded credit, and other circumstances.

In 1833, President Jackson, who opposed the Bank of the United States, ordered that the public deposits held by it, amounting to some $37,000,000, be transferred to eighty selected local banks in various parts of the country. These banks soon came to regard this money almost as a permanent deposit, and, upon the strength of it, poured forth volumes of paper currency.

It was a period of swift and splendid national development. The lakes and rivers of the country teemed with steamboats. Stephenson's loco-

---

[1] The bank charters of those days were largely "based upon ignorance, intrigue, favoritism, or corruption." James Buchanan thus characterized the Bank of the United States: "It has defied Congress, violated the laws, and is mixed up in politics."

motive, "The Rocket," had firmly established the practicability of steam travel and transportation by rail, and the eleven hundred miles of railway in operation in 1835 were destined to be doubled, each five years, until 1860. Coal displaced wood as fuel. New towns and cities marked the outburst of progress. Chicago, which was only a frontier post in 1832, became in six years a flourishing town, having eight steamers connecting it with Buffalo.

Under these conditions credit expanded prodigiously, and a frenzy of speculation fell upon the people. There were great land "booms" in Maine and throughout the West, and the sterling simplicities of life were forgotten in dreams of quickly acquired wealth without labor. Imports, in 1836, exceeded exports by more than fifty million dollars, which called for specie. The day of reckoning was at hand.

In 1835, the President announced to Congress that the public debt was extinguished, and urged legislation in regard to the disposition of the surplus. A law was therefore passed in 1836 withdrawing the scattered millions of specie from the banks, for the purpose of distributing it among the States. Sales of the public lands had increased from about $3,000,000 in 1831, to $25,000,000 in 1836, and the President, who seemed resolved to smash things and leave the repairs to his successor, now ordered that hence-forth only coin should be received for them.

People at once awoke to realize that they had "been a-riding in a balloon, and the gas was out." A heavy decline in the price of cotton and other exports increased the troubles. The Bank of the United States, and most other banks, suspended. Nearly everybody failed. Notes were worthless, loans unpaid, confidence utterly destroyed. Some States repudiated their obligations, and the General Government was in peril of bankruptcy. It was a dismal time. Stay laws were hastily passed, and American credit received a shock from which it did not fully recover for many years.[1]

The panic of 1857 burst upon the country like a tempest from a clear sky. California had poured into the lap of the world over four hun-dred millions of gold during the seven preced-

---

[1] It was estimated that the panic of 1837–39 caused 33,000 failures, involving a loss of $450,000,000.

ing years, and her yield in 1857 was fifty-five
millions.   Immigrants had been coming to our
shores at the rate of a thousand or more a day,
and, avoiding slave soil, had swarmed upon our
Western lands.

The harvest of the preceding year was one
of the finest ever garnered.   Our carrying trade
was increasing; factories were nowhere idle.
There was no governmental exigency, no popular discontent.   The telegraph had been brought
into general use, and a great mileage of railway
had been recently completed, or was under construction.   The conditions of life were changing
with bewildering rapidity.   Prices were high
and advancing, and there was a prodigious expansion of credit.

But with the coming of summer there was a
vague uneasiness in the air, which soon grew
into distrustful apprehension.   Banks carefully
scrutinized their collateral, and called in loans,
and prudent merchants set their houses in order.

On the 24th of August the Ohio Life Insurance and Trust Company failed.   This was a
large institution, located by its charter in Cin-
cinnati, but its chief business was banking in

New York, where its cashier resided. He had borrowed several millions on call, upon securities which could not be turned into cash when demand was made for the return of the loans.

This event was the panic signal, and the public confidence at once gave way to fright. Within a few days, prices fell fifty per cent upon the Stock Exchange. Everybody wanted money, but it was impossible to realize upon any kind of property, except at a disastrous sacrifice. Many houses failed, and within a few weeks the banks of New York and other cities suspended payments.

The effects of the panic of 1857 were widely and profoundly felt, but recovery was comparatively rapid. It was generally thought to have been caused by the inflation of credit, over-trading, and speculation.

The great Civil War began with the surrender of Fort Sumter, April 14th, 1861. Specie payments were generally suspended throughout the United States on the 30th of December, 1861, because of the issue of paper currency by the Government for war purposes. Commercial dealings with the Southern States were entirely cut off. The surrender of Lee to Grant, April 9th, 1865, practically ended the war, and the issue of greenbacks ceased.

The country now resolutely set itself to the task of grappling with its huge war debt, and before all the soldiers had been sent home it was reduced $30,000,000. As might naturally be expected, there were some financial and business disturbances at this juncture.[1]

In the spring of 1866, Overend, Gurney & Co., one of the largest and most influential firms in Europe, suspended payment. This house stood next to the Bank of England as a tower of financial strength, and was known all over the world. This, and other events, produced stagnation and distress for a time, but its effects were not very seriously or extensively felt in this country.

Some years of rapid material progress fol-

---

[1] The national debt was, in 1857, twenty-eight millions; in 1860, sixty-five millions; in 1861, ninety-one millions; in 1862, five hundred and fourteen millions; in 1863, eleven hundred and twenty millions; in 1864, eighteen hundred and sixteen millions. In August, 1865, it reached twenty-eight hundred and forty-five millions, which was the maximum. Specie payments were not resumed until January 1, 1879.

lowed this epoch, notwithstanding that the people insisted upon paying the National debt as fast as possible. It seemed that, in passing through the terrible war, the Nation awoke for the first time to a full realizing sense of its greatness, its strength, and its resources, and all the arts of peace now sprang forward with amazing elasticity. Prosperity was general, at least throughout the Northern States. Productive and transportation facilities were greatly increased. The country was busy with its industries.

The period around 1870 is remarkable for its railway construction, which opened up large areas of new territory to settlement.[1] But much capital was absorbed in these enterprises, many of which proved unproductive. Money grew scarce, interest high, and times hard. The collapse of the "building mania" in Vienna, in 1873, was followed by financial troubles throughout Europe.

The American crisis came, in September of this "bad year," with the failure of Jay Cooke

---

[1] 4,615 miles of railway were built in 1869; 6,070 in 1870, and 7,379 miles in 1871.

& Co. The head of this house had been the financial agent of the Government during the war, for the sale of its. bonds, and more than $2,000,000,000 had passed through his hands. He afterward became financial agent for the Northern Pacific Railway, and his failure followed this connection.

The country was flooded with securities, and other failures came swiftly. Eighty-three railway companies suspended payment, and the New York Stock Exchange found it expedient to close its doors from the 18th to the 30th of September.

All industries were affected. Commodities declined in price; factories in all parts of the country were closed down, because their products were unsalable, and great numbers of people were thrown out of employment.

Several grim and weary years elapsed before . this industrial paralysis passed away. In fact, many believe this panic to have been more grievous than any which preceded it, because its results were of such long duration.

Enormous speculative enterprises came again with the advent of prosperity, and reached their climax in 1880–81, when a movement toward lower prices for railway securities set in, owing to competition in rates, and stock manipulations. In 1883, warehouses were crowded with goods, gold was being drawn away from the country, and failures were somewhat numerous.[1]

In May, 1884, the New York house of Grant & Ward failed disastrously, with liabilities of $17,000,000, and several New York city banks suspended. Other failures followed, and for a time intense anxiety prevailed. But the city banks formed a syndicate for mutual protection and support, and the general distrust soon died away. This crisis was more severe in New York than elsewhere. It may, in fact, be called a panic in securities, which affected speculators and financiers more than those in trade.

---

[1] Railway construction in 1880 reached 7,174 miles; in 1881, 11,142 miles; in 1882, 10,821 miles; in 1883, 6,400 miles.

CHAPTER XII.

THE PANIC OF 1893.

THE most severe and extensive panic, in many respects, which has ever afflicted this nation, was that of 1893. No section of the country has escaped its ravages, nor any industry its blighting effects, and the spell of its influence has not yet passed away. It cannot fairly be imputed to over-trading and speculation, and it sprang neither from too much nor too little currency in circulation. It will, however, pass into financial history as a "currency panic," from the fact that its proximate cause was distrust of the stability of the currency, which produced a demand for our gold, and caused a general contraction of credit.

But numerous events, here and elsewhere, have certainly assisted, more or less directly, to pave the way for, and intensify, this great crisis. Among these may be noted the depreciation of silver throughout the world, and the attendant decline in the prices of staple products, the bankruptcy of some foreign nations, and the increased financial difficulties of others, the scandalous failure of the Panama Canal project, the collapse of the house of Baring Brothers & Co., the Australian bank failures, the suspension of silver coinage in India, our own tariff uncertainties, and the condition of the public Treasury.

The five years from 1888 to 1892, inclusive, comprised a period of fair prosperity in the United States. Crops averaged satisfactorily, the volume of business was large, and labor was well employed. But speculation, as a rule, was only moderate on the exchanges, there was a constant decline in the prices of commodities, and competition was excessively sharp in all lines of business. It was a period of severe trial for small capitalists, and mercantile failures were numerous.[1]

---

[1] Commercial Failures.   Liabilities.

1888............10,679	............$123,829,973
1889............10,882	148,784,337
1890............10,907	189,856,964
1891............12,273	189,868,638
1892............10,344	114,044,167
1893............15,242	346,779,889
1894............13,885	172,992,856

—Dun's Review.

One of the most important economic questions of modern times relates to the circulating medium, or currency.

With the progress of civilization, the vastly increased production of commodities, the quickened intercourse between nations, and the multiplied appliances of credit, there has come also a monetary evolution. Among barbarous people, wampum and cowry shells serve as a medium of exchange; but the tendency is, as wealth and knowledge increase, to adopt a more substantial, convenient, and valuable form of money. For many centuries, therefore, the more enlightened races have used gold and silver.

Owing, however, to the constantly increasing difficulty of keeping these two metals at a parity of value, or from "parting company" in their relative values, and the fact that payments will always be made in the least valuable currency —in virtue of the law that "bad money drives out good money," the most important commercial countries have, one after another, closed their mints to silver, and adopted a gold standard. The result has been that the annually increasing surplus of silver has "glutted and cloyed all markets." [1]

This mighty measure of alleged contraction has not been accomplished without much opposition. It is stoutly maintained that money owners, and creditor nations like England, have been benefited, while agricultural, industrial, and commercial interests throughout the world have correspondingly suffered.

It has been followed by a great reduction in nominal values, by frequent trade depressions and financial revulsions, and by the bankruptcy of several debtor nations.

As the United States is the leading silver-producing country of the world, there has naturally been a strong and widespread feeling averse to the demonetization of the white metal by our Government, and the policy pursued for many years was a waiting one. In 1873, however, the Government ceased to coin silver on private

---

[1] This would probably have occurred long ago but for the fact that the populous East has absorbed such prodigious quantities of silver from the Western nations. Humboldt observes that silver has always moved in a direction opposite to the movement of civilization.

account, and made preparation to return to a gold standard, thus practically demonetizing silver. But in 1878 the passage of the Bland Bill once more made silver a legal tender, and reestablished the double, or bimetallic standard.[1]

But the friends of silver became dissatisfied with this measure. It did not go far enough. New mines of the metal, and new and improved processes for its extraction, were being constantly discovered and developed, and its production correspondingly waxed in quantity, while it waned in value, as compared with gold.

---

[1] The Bland, or Bland-Allison Bill imposed upon the Secretary of the Treasury the duty of purchasing silver bullion and coining at least two million dollars every month, each to weigh 412½ grains, the same to be legal tender. This bill passed the Senate by a vote of 48 to 21. It became a law over the President's veto.

The bill had the support of both Senators from Pennsylvania, Ohio, Indiana, Illinois, Wisconsin, Nebraska, and Minnesota. Of those opposed, seven were Democrats and fourteen Republicans. Among the Democrats were Bayard of Delaware, Kernan of New York, Whyte of Maryland, and McPherson of New Jersey. Among the Republicans were James G. Blaine and Roscoe Conkling, Morrill and Edmunds, of Vermont, and both Republican Senators from Massachusetts, New Hampshire, and Rhode Island. One California senator voted against the bill, the other in favor of it.

The Government was pledged to maintain parity between its coinage of both metals, and additional pressure was brought to bear that, as the mint was open to the free coinage of gold, so also it should be opened to the free coinage of silver. Happily, wiser counsels prevailed, and the country escaped the task of carrying the silver of the world—a burden too heavy for the shoulders of any single nation.

It was at length proposed, as an alternative— which the free-coinage advocates hoped would be but temporary—that the Government should purchase silver bullion, and hold it as a basis for the issue of paper currency. This project was rendered more plausible by the great reduction in the National debt, and the gradual retirement of the bonds which serve as a basis and security for the currency issues of the National banks.[1]

There was much opposition, but in the summer of 1890, under the exigencies of party poli-

---

[1] From July 1st, 1884, to July 1st, 1893, the National debt was reduced 586 millions of dollars. (The Director of the United States Mint reports the silver money of the world as $3,820,571,346 ; the gold money as $3,727,018,-869.)

12

tics, the Sherman Bill became a law.   This enactment directed the Secretary of the Treasury
to purchase each month 4,500,000 ounces of
silver bullion, and to issue against it legal-
tender notes, payable "in coin."

This measure is held by many as immediately
responsible for the panic of 1893.   It is alleged
to have impaired confidence, at home and abroad,
in the stability and soundness of our currency,
incited the withdrawal and prevented the inflow
of foreign capital, plunged the nation into uncertainty and apprehension of the future,
checked enterprise and investment, and brought
paralysis upon all our industries.'

The early effect of the Sherman law was ap-
parently to impart a degree of buoyancy to business and advance the price of securities, although the latter was in part, if not chiefly, due
to large railway earnings and easy money.   It
was generally believed that this silver legislation would enhance nominal values through

---

' The total value of all the silver purchased by the
Government under both the Bland and Sherman laws is
but a fraction of the loss which they are believed to
have caused ; a striking commentary on the worth of
confidence and credit.

inflation of the currency.   Our harvests in 1890
were disappointing, and in the fall months came
shrinkage of prices and depression.[1]

The year 1889 had been one of the most flourishing years in the commercial history of Great
Britain.   Good things were going in various
parts of the globe, and " John Bull," with his
jingling gold, had secured a full share of them.

But along in the autumn of 1890 it suddenly
transpired that the great London house of Baring Brothers and Co. must fail disastrously,
unless it could at once receive material aid.   Its
inability to meet its obligations, amounting to
upward of a hundred and forty million dollars,
was chiefly owing to investments in the Argentine Republic, which had been widely bulletined
as "the finest undeveloped country in the
world."

In this emergency, Mr. William Lidderdale,
Governor of the Bank of England, secured from
a syndicate of great London houses a guarantee

---

[1] Many large industrial corporations were organized
during the year 1890.   Notably the H. B. Claflin Co.,
J. P. Coats' Thread Works, American Tobacco Co.,
Proctor & Gamble Co., etc.   The McKinley Tariff Bill
went into operation on the 6th of October.

of protection against loss, to the extent of four million pounds sterling, if it would undertake to liquidate the Barings' estate, and, from the British Government, authority to issue seven million pounds sterling of notes to facilitate the matter. The Bank therefore assumed, on the 15th of September, the task of meeting the Barings' engagements, to the amount of twenty-eight million five hundred thousand pounds sterling. It was said that this action prevented the culmination of what "would have proved the most terrible panic recorded in history'.

The crisis was averted, but the business world was stirred to its depths, and general confidence was but slowly restored. What English writers described as a "semi-panic" existed for many

---

[1] In recognition of his services at this juncture, Mr. Lidderdale received the thanks of his Government, and the freedom of the city of London. The successful liquidation of the Barings' Estate has since fully justified the wisdom of his course. The paper signed by the parties to this great transaction is interesting as a model of brevity and simplicity ; it was as follows :

"In consideration of advances which the Bank of England has agreed to make to Baring Brothers & Co., to enable them to discharge at maturity their liabilities existing on the night of November 15th, we, the undersigned, hereby agree, each individual, firm, or company

months in London, and this, together with de-
bates in Congress upon the silver question,
caused foreign investors to return to us large
quantities of securities which, under our low
bank reserves and money pressure, fell heavily.
The North River Bank, of New York city, went
into the hands of a receiver, and there were
numerous failures; but the manufacturing and
mercantile interests of the country were not so
much disturbed as to excite general apprehension.

Bank statements, in 1891, revealed a considerably improved condition of affairs.   Bountiful
harvests, in face of scant crops in other countries, helped greatly to restore confidence and
advance prices, despite the possibilities of silver

---

for himself, or themselves alone, and to the amount set
opposite his or their names respectively, to make good
any loss, whenever the Bank of England shall determine
that the final liquidation of the liabilities of Baring
Brothers & Co. has been completed, so far as in the
opinion of the Governors is practicable.   All the
guarantors shall contribute ratably, and no one individual, firm, or company shall be called on for his or
their contribution without a like call being made on the
others.   The maximum period over which such liquidation may extend is three years, commencing November 15th.

legislation. A still larger volume of business was transacted in 1892, and failures were less numerous and important than in the year preceding. Bank clearances exceeded those of 1891 by nearly ten per cent. But crops, and especially that of cotton, were short, and the fact was reflected in railway earnings, and in exports. There was increasing agitation of the silver question, a growing disposition abroad to drop American securities, and an alarming outflow of gold.

The year 1893 opened with gray skies.   Prices of everything were low and falling, and though trade continued fairly active, there was little sale for commercial paper.   During the first two months of the year our exports exceeded imports by thirty-six million dollars, yet gold was rapidly leaving the country, and the Treasury reserve as steadily declining—a fact which caused much anxiety.   Failures during the first quarter were more numerous than for the same period in many preceding years.

Large amounts of capital had, year after year, been sent from England to the banks in Australia for investment.   Most of these banks had

branches throughout the country, a dozen sometimes existing in a locality which could not
offer legitimate business enough to support
even one. There was much competition between them, and as English money was plentiful, it easily found its way into all sorts of
speculative enterprises, such as mines, railway
and irrigation companies, sheep and ostrich
farms, etc.

This bubble was pricked early in 1893, when,
from January 15th to May 15th, fourteen banks
failed, with liabilities of nearly $500,000,000.
The event did not create a notable panic in London, but it was another severe shock to confidence, and it made money more stringent. The
effect upon trade, on both sides of the Atlantic,
was depressing.

As the popular anxiety and uncertainty continued to increase, President Cleveland announced, on the 20th of April, that he had determined "to preserve the parity between gold and
silver, and between all obligations of the Government." On the sixth day of June, he declared
that "Congress must deal with the currency
question, the condition of which is the only

menace to the country's welfare and prosperity."[1]

By June there were runs upon banks in various parts of the country, and an alarming number of failures. Prices continued to droop upon the stagnant exchanges, and there soon came an embarrassing scarcity of currency. People were hoarding it. The banks of New York city rallied for mutual support, and authorized the issue of clearing-house certificates. The same thing was done in Philadelphia. It proved a helpful measure.

On the 27th of June, it was announced that the Government of India had suspended free silver coinage, and determined upon a gold standard. There was an instant fall in the price of silver all over the world. Three days later, the President convened Congress, in extra session, for the 7th of August.

---

[1] The total net gold exports, during the first six months of 1893, were $61,958,895, as follows:

January	$12,213,553
February	12,988,068
March	1,504,991
April	18,344,979
May	15,205,760
June	1,701,544

Confidence was now so badly wilted that its revival seemed almost hopeless. The number of banks which suspended during July and August was unprecedented in the history of the country, and numerous railway companies, and other large corporations, became bankrupt. A large proportion of the manufacturing concerns of the country closed down, or curtailed their hours of labor. Great numbers of people were thrown out of employment, and there was widespread distress.

Congress met on the 7th of August, and all eyes in the land were eagerly turned towards Washington. On the 28th of August, the House voted to repeal the Sherman law by a majority of 131, and there was an instant rebound of hope and confidence.

But repeal was fiercely resisted by a powerful and adroit faction in the Senate, and for two months that august body debated, and "preserved its traditions," while industry languished, and the people suffered.

At length a bill passed both houses of Congress, and became a law on the first day of November, 1893, which provides, not for the demonetization of silver, but for the repeal of so much of the Sherman Act as required the purchase of silver bullion by the Government.

It was hoped and expected that a revival of business would follow this legislation, but it had less effect than was anticipated. The silver market in Europe responded but slightly. Shipments of gold continued. There was no maintained advance in the price of securities or commodities. Confidence did not return; the waters had been too deeply troubled.

There were fewer mercantile failures during 1893 than might naturally have been expected under the conditions which prevailed, although the proportion of those failing *in good credit* is given as fully four times that in preceding normal years. The manner in which manufacturers, and merchants generally withstood the strain bears witness that, as a rule, they were in a sound and conservative position.

The year 1894 was a period of extraordinary depression in all departments of industry. Several times during the year there was a tendency toward improvement; but the deficient revenues of the Government—which twice compelled the issue of fifty millions of bonds, the heavy gold exports, the low prices of our products, tariff uncertainties, the wrangle over the proposition to "coin the seigniorage," fears of "free silver" legislation, the revolutionary labor troubles, and other events, constantly deferred the return of confidence, and arrested the revival of trade.[1]

In April and May came disastrous floods in the Middle States, the strike of the Connellsville coke-workers, the Coxey armies of tramps, the

---

[1] "The gold exports are themselves the evidence of the destruction of confidence, for on the basis of our ordinary trade requirements there could be no need for gold shipments, as .he excess of exports of merchandise and silver for the twelve months ending November 30, 1894 amounted to the large sum of $211,932,000. In face of this large trade balance, we were obliged to ship in the same twelve months no less than $73,704,000 gold, net, making the total excess of exports almost three hundred million dollars ($285,636,000).

Low prices nearly everywhere were a striking characteristic of the year, accentuating the depression, while at the same time aggravating it. The price of wheat several times got down to below 55 cents a bushel in New York ; cotton sold at 5½ cents a pound in November ; print cloths got down to 2⅜ cents a yard. Besides this, we might mention various other articles and commodities which sold at extremely low quotations, such as iron, steel, sugar, etc."—*Commercial and Financial Chronicle.*

bituminous coal-miners' strike, which rendered it necessary to call out the militia in eight or ten States, and the resulting "coal famine." The event of June and July was the great and stormy strike of the American Railway Union to enforce the demands of the Pullman employees. Government expenditures, for the fiscal year ending July 1st, 1894, were about $70,000,-000 in excess of the revenue.

On the 8th of August, the gold balance in the Treasury stood at $52,189,500, the lowest figure of the year. The enactment of the Tariff Bill, which went into effect on the 28th of August, at once increased the revenues of the Government, and imparted some life to business. In September there was a better demand for goods, stimulated by needs for consumption, and some hopeful signs of slowly returning prosperity. There were no new disturbing developments, and a decreasing number of failures. Production was expanding.

But again, in December, the outflow of gold was heavy, large shipments being made each week through the month, and the "bad year of 1894" closed with drooping markets.

It became painfully evident in January, 1895, that the gold reserve in the Treasury must again be replenished. Another issue of Government bonds was therefore sold, in February, to a syndicate of bankers, who contracted to import gold, and to maintain such rates for foreign exchange as to render further exports of the metal unprofitable. It proved a felicitous and masterful stroke of policy.

It seems now to have been the turning-point in the great panic. The ebbing tide of gold was at once checked, and the general movement of affairs put to the right-about. Hope revived; confidence grew. Depression gave way to enthusiasm. Securities, iron, wheat, cotton, all the staples, advanced rapidly.

It is impossible to predict what the future may bring, but up to this time, (August), nothing has transpired to hinder the full return of prosperity. The demand for labor increases; wages advance; business improves; crops promise fairly well. Money is abundant, and interest low, with every prospect that it will long remain so. Belief has become general that industrial interests are at last coming up out of the wilderness of evil days, and now face toward piping times. The menacing clouds remaining in the horizon are the scant revenue of the Government and the condition of the National Treasury, uncertainty regarding silver legislation, and the currency question.

It is alleged that the Bland and Sherman laws have brought upon the Government a loss of nearly two hundred millions, and upon the people panic, deprivation, and distress. But they were circumscribed in their powers for evil, because they authorized the issue of silver coin and currency only within certain limits.

But it is to these limitations alone that the partisans of silver ascribe the mischief. We are asked to believe that if these enactments had but sanctioned *unlimited* silver coinage, they would have proved fountains of boundless prosperity, instead of panic-breeders. This is to say, that if we merely put our hands into the fire they may be burned, but if we plunge in all over we shall remain cool, comfortable, and happy.

It is from texts like this that a multitude of mining colonels, politicians, populists, and quibbling demagogues seeking to ride to power and plunder upon any specious fad that offers, have been preaching in the crusade for free silver coinage. They are, in reality, attempting to manufacture sufficient votes to force fifty cents' worth of silver upon the people, as the lawful equivalent of a dollar's worth of gold.

Their success would banish gold from circulation, and the price of commodities would soon be adjusted to the value of silver as bullion. Two Mexican silver dollars can now be obtained in exchange for one stamped with the American Eagle, because our Government is pledged to redeem the latter in gold. But when the Government shall no longer maintain parity between its coinage of gold and silver, the Mexican dollar will be more valuable than ours, because it contains more silver.

It were better that we call half-a-bushel a bushel, and half-a-yard a yard, than half-a-dollar's worth of silver a dollar. This nation must have an honest unit of value, first, last, and all the time.

The campaign in behalf of " Free Silver" has been conducted with vigor and shrewdness, but, thanks to the press and the platform, light is at last reaching the farmers who have grain to sell, the five million depositors in savings banks, the wage and salary earners, and all good citizens up and down the land who read and think. They are fast learning that free silver coinage is a delusion and a snare, and the danger that the nation may be plunged into its mad confusion is constantly decreasing.

Silver is an old and faithful servant, but commerce has outgrown its use, except as subsidiary coin. That the great nations will unite to reinstate it is altogether improbable.[1] Bimetallism has become a "back number." For the United

---

[1] The first International Monetary Conference was that of June, 1867, held, on invitation of the French Government, in Paris, "to consider the question of uniformity of coinage, and to seek for the basis of ulterior negotiations." The United States, and eighteen of the principal countries of Europe, were represented. The conference voted unanimously against the adoption, by the countries, of the silver standard; and unanimously, with the exception of the Netherlands, in favor of the single gold standard.

The second International Monetary Conference was called by the United States, and held at Paris in 1878. Germany refused to send delegates, but twelve countries were represented. It was the opinion of the delegates,

States alone to sanction unlimited silver coinage at any ratio with gold which the friends of silver would approve, would be to open upon the country a Pandora's box of evils. The most enlightened opinion now holds that the world has reached a stage in its progress where gold and silver can no longer be forced to bear any fixed relation to each other as standard measures and representatives of value, and that the best interests of mankind now require the adoption of the rarer, more valuable, and

---

that the use of gold and silver as money should be left to the discretion of each state, or group of states.

The third such conference, that of 1881, was called by France and the United States, " to examine and adopt, for the purpose of submitting the same to the governments represented, a plan and a system for the re-establishment of the use of gold and silver as bimetallic money, according to a settled value between those metals." Nineteen countries were represented, but the conference adjourned without practical results.

The fourth, and last, International Monetary Conference met at Brussels in 1892. It was called by the Government of the United States, "for the purpose of conferring as to what measures, if any, can be taken to increase the use of silver as money in the currency system of nations." Twenty countries were represented at this conference, but it adjourned without definite practical conclusions.

more stable gold as the universal foundation money.

With the progress which is anticipated for the coming century, along all lines of thought and industry, will a way be found to prevent panics?

We cannot, of course, foresee coming conditions, but, as the causes of panics and their remedies are in the keeping chiefly of those who suffer from them, it seems not unreasonable to expect that their prevention may be among the social and economic victories of the future. It may, at least, be confidently predicted, that if their recurrence cannot be entirely obviated or suppressed, their power for mischief will be curbed—that as the world gains experience and wisdom, panics will become less frequent, less severe, and of shorter duration.

Yet there are those who contend that panics will continue to come and go as in times past, in virtue of some vast purpose, some principle of rhythmic ebb and flow involved in the unfolding plan of evolution. They argue that, as the law that all must die rules over all causes of death, so, under law, panics must inevitably accompany commercial activity, independently of desultory events held to be their proximate causes, such as good or bad crops, the policy of political parties, or even the caprices of human nature.

It may be so, but we, practical people, can hardly accept such theories. Yet we, too, believe in the reign of absolute law, such, for example, as that which governs the running of a watch. If it is badly constructed, if there is sand among its cogs, or its wheels get askew, it will not keep time until it is repaired and adjusted. In other words, we believe in the law that effect follows cause, and that the former will be differentiated as we modify the latter.

If we may at all judge the future by the past, the panics that lie along the course of affairs will prove beacon-lights of warning and instruction.

They teach, among other things, that it is not law but labor that creates value, and that the dollar, the unit of value, must be rigorously measured by the average amount of intelligence, capital, and labor required to produce its metal.   And furthermore, that a baseless, or too much expanded paper currency, is sure to prove a treacherous stimulus, which will leave in its wake depression, disorder, and insolvency.

They give grounds for the conclusion that the notion of a so-called "elastic currency," or one which will automatically expand and contract according to the needs of the people, is a fallacy, because the inherent force of money makes only for expansion.   The kite must have a tail.

A study of panics will suggest to the vigilant and cautious business man that he should be on the lookout for a sudden change of popular sentiment after a lengthened period of general prosperity and expansion of credit.

He will observe that the conditions which have usually preceded a panic were something as follows: speculation active, labor well employed, immigration heavy, stocks, commodities, and especially iron and its products have advanced regularly in price, and become stationary or top-heavy.   Luxury and expenditure flourish, and the pace of everything is swift.

Bank statements show large amounts of loans and discounts, and decreasing deposits.

When, on the other hand, the panic has passed, and the end of liquidation has come, when prices have touched bottom and begin to rebound, when idle workmen find employment, when bank statements show increasing deposits and a healthy demand for discounts, and the general stringency of expenditure is relaxed, he will naturally conclude that conditions indicate a return of confidence, a rapid resumption of prosperous business, and an upward movement, which will probably last from two to four years, with comparative safety in extending credit.

APPENDIX.

ASSIGNMENT, INSOLVENT, EXEMPTION, AND OTHER LAWS OF ALL THE STATES AND TERRITORIES.

ALABAMA.—Has no distinct insolvent or assignment law, but assignments can be made at common law. There can be no preferences in a general assignment. Acceptance of a dividend under assignment does not discharge debtor. Twenty years bar actions upon judgments. Six years bar actions for money loaned, stated accounts, or promise in writing. Three years bar open accounts. LEGAL INTEREST, eight per cent. EXEMPTIONS: Homestead of house and lot in town, or one hundred and sixty acres in the country, in either case not to exceed two thousand dollars in value; also personal property to the value of one thousand dollars, certain specified articles, and wages to the amount of twenty-five dollars per month.

ARIZONA.—Has no insolvent law. Five years bar actions on judgments; four years bar contracts in writing; two years if not in writing. EXEMPTIONS: The homestead not exceeding in value five thousand dollars, and certain specified articles to the value of six hundred dollars. LEGAL INTEREST, ten per cent.

ARKANSAS.—Has an assignment law for the benefit of creditors which permits preferences. It does not discharge the debtor from his obligations without unanimous consent of the creditors, nor does it affect the claims of those who do not come into the assignment. LIMITATIONS OF ACTIONS : On accounts, three years ; notes and sealed instruments, five years ; on judgments, ten years. LEGAL INTEREST, six per cent. EXEMPTIONS : For head of a family, outside of any town or city, one hundred and sixty acres of land, not to exceed twenty-five hundred dollars in value, or not less than eighty acres without regard to value. In city or town not exceeding one acre, of the value of twenty-five hundred dollars, or not less than one-fourth of an acre without regard to value ; also, for the head of a family, personal property to the value of five hundred dollars. For a single person, two hundred dollars' worth of personal property besides wearing apparel.

CALIFORNIA.—Has an insolvent law, which does not permit preferences, but under which the debtor may be discharged from obligations incurred in the State to citizens of the State. Non-resident creditors, who do not voluntarily become parties to the proceedings, can retain their claims against the debtor. LIMITATIONS : Actions must be commenced within five years on the judgment or decree of a court ; within four years on a promissory note, contract, or obligation in writing, executed in the State ; within two years upon any contract or obligation not in writing. Seven per cent is legal interest. Interest cannot be collected on open accounts. EXEMPTIONS : The homestead (under certain conditions), not exceeding in value five thousand dollars ; the cabin or dwelling of a miner, not exceeding five hundred dollars in value, and a list of specified articles necessary, or applicable, to the trade or calling of the debtor. Days of grace are not allowed on bills of exchange or promissory notes.

COLORADO.—Has an assignment law, which does not permit preferences, and does not discharge the debtor without the unanimous consent of his creditors. The claims of creditors who do not come into an assignment are secondary to those filed within three months after assignee has mailed notice of assignment, unless creditors can show that they did not receive such notice. LIMITATIONS OF ACTIONS: Execution may issue on a judgment for ten years from its entry, but it is then considered as satisfied unless revived. Actions for debt founded upon contract or liability in action must be brought within six years. EXEMPTIONS: Tools and stock in trade, used in carrying on business, to the value of two hundred dollars; library and implements of any professional man, not exceeding three hundred dollars. Wearing apparel, and specified articles. LEGAL INTEREST, eight per cent.

CONNECTICUT.—Has an insolvent law, but the debtor is not permitted to make a preferential assignment. If his estate pays seventy per cent on all claims that have been proved, he will receive his discharge in full for such claims only; all other claims hold good against his property after the expiration of two years from his discharge. EXEMPTIONS: Necessary wearing apparel, bedding, and furniture. Implements of the debtor's trade, and certain specified articles; the land and dwelling actually occupied by the owner, to the value of one thousand dollars, provided he has recorded his declaration to the effect that it is his homestead. STATUTE OF LIMITATIONS bars action on contract under seal, or non-negotiable note, after seventeen years; on account, book debt, simple contract, writing not under seal, or negotiable notes, six years; express contracts, of which there is no written memorandum, three years. LEGAL INTEREST in the State, six per cent.

DELAWARE.—Has an assignment law, which does not permit preferences in cases of insolvency, nor does it permit the discharge of the debtor unless the creditors severally agree to release. The rights of creditors who do not come into an assignment are not affected by the assignment, but they will lose their dividends. LIMITATIONS OF ACTIONS: Accounts, three years; notes, six years. Judgments presumed paid in twenty years unless rebutted. A verbal promise to pay a debt will, if proved, revive it. LEGAL INTEREST, six per cent; penalty for usury, forfeiture of a sum equal to the amount loaned. EXEMPTIONS permitted in this State are small and they vary in the different counties.

DISTRICT OF COLUMBIA.—Preferences in an assignment are void, and all debts are payable *pro rata*. EXEMPTIONS: Household furniture and wearing apparel of a householder are exempt except for servant's or laborer's wages due, to the amount of three hundred dollars; provisions and fuel for three months; mechanic's tools or implements, of any trade, to the value of two hundred dollars, with stock to the same amount; library and implements of a professional man, to the value of three hundred dollars; farmers' team and utensils to the value of one hundred dollars; family pictures and library, to the value of four hundred dollars. LIMITATION, OF ACTIONS: Actions must be brought within three years on simple contracts, book accounts, notes, etc. Twelve years is the limit on specialties. LEGAL INTEREST, six per cent.

FLORIDA.—A general assignment law exists, which does not permit preferences, but which expressly discharges the debtor if he complies with its provisions. It is believed, however, that such discharge is void, if the creditor does not reside in the State, and the contract was neither made nor to be performed therein. Creditors who do not come into an assignment lose their dividends. EXEMPTIONS: Homestead of one hundred and sixty acres of land and improvements, if in the country; a residence and business house and one-half acre of ground, if in a town or city, together with a thousand dollars' worth of personal property. LIMITATIONS OF ACTIONS: Accounts, four years; notes and other unsealed instruments, five years. Judgments, bonds, and notes under seal, twenty years. LEGAL INTEREST, eight per cent.

GEORGIA.—Has an assignment law (the act of 1880–81), which permits preferences under conditions, but the unanimous consent of creditors is necessary to the insolvent's discharge. Creditors who do not come into the assignment simply lose the dividend that may be declared. EXEMPTIONS: Homestead of realty or personality, or both, to the value in the aggregate of sixteen hundred dollars. LIMITATIONS OF ACTIONS: Upon open accounts, four years; notes, etc., six years; sealed instruments, twenty years. Judgments must have execution issued thereon within seven years, or they become dormant. Dormant judgment may be revived within three years. LEGAL INTEREST, eight per cent.

IDAHO.—LIMITATIONS OF ACTIONS: Instruments in writing, five years; contract or liability, not founded in writing, including accounts, two years. EXEMPTIONS: Homestead, consisting of dwelling-house thereon and its appurtenances, not exceeding in value five thousand dollars, to be selected by the husband and wife, or either of them, or other head of family (the usual declaration must be made and recorded). A single person may claim a homestead, not to exceed one thousand dollars in value. There are, besides, many articles specified as exempt. LEGAL INTEREST, ten per cent.

ILLINOIS.—Has an assignment law, which permits no preferences. Acceptance of dividends does not discharge the debtor. Creditors who do not come in waive claim to the assets assigned. INTEREST: five per cent is allowed when no rate is specified. LIMITATIONS OF ACTIONS: Five years upon accounts, unwritten contracts, and for injury to property; upon bonds, notes, bills of exchange, leases, and other written contracts, ten years. All other actions, including action on judgments of other States, five years.

INDIANA.—Has a distinct assignment law, which does not, in a *general* assignment, permit preferences, but a special assignment may be made to secure particular creditors. Unanimous consent of creditors is necessary to discharge the debtor. Creditors who do not come into an assignment merely lose their share of the assets assigned. LIMITATIONS OF ACTIONS: On accounts and contracts not in writing, within six years. On promissory notes, bills of exchange, and other written contracts for the payment of money, within ten years. On judgments of a court of record, twenty years. EXEMPTIONS: Any resident householder has an exemption from levy and sale, under execution or attachment, of real or personal property, or both, as he may select, to the value of six hundred dollars. The law further provides that no property shall be sold, by virtue of an execution, for less than two-thirds of its appraised cash value. This provision may, however, be waived, by inserting in the note or contract: "Payable without relief from valuation or appraisement laws." But the right to exemption cannot be waived by contract. LEGAL INTEREST, eight per cent.

INDIAN TERRITORY.—ASSIGNMENTS: By Act of Congress, the statute of Arkansas applies to this Territory. EXEMPTIONS and LIMITATIONS, as written in Mansfield's Digest of the State of Arkansas (1884), apply to this Territory. LEGAL INTEREST, on open accounts, made in the Territory, six per cent. If not made there, rate is fixed by the law of the State where made. Contracts draw rate contracted for, unless the rate is usurious in the State where the contract is made. Land cannot be sold under executions. Judgments must be satisfied from personal property.

IOWA.—Has a general assignment law, which does not permit preferences; but independent of this law, and before assignment, preferences to creditors are allowed, if in good faith. The unanimous consent of creditors is required for the debtor's discharge. Creditors who do not come into the assignment do not receive a dividend from the assets. Their claims remain unimpaired. LIMITATIONS OF ACTIONS: Accounts, five years; notes and written instruments, ten years; judgments, twenty years. The failure to account for goods consigned is embezzlement. LEGAL INTEREST, six per cent. EXEMPTIONS: Homestead used as a residence by the owner, not exceeding half an acre in extent, if within a town plot (or if not, it must not embrace more than forty acres) with other specified personal property.

KANSAS.—Has an assignment law, which operates only to distribute the debtor's property ratably among all his creditors who prove their claims, but it does not discharge him from his debts. Creditors who do not come in do not participate in the assigned property, but their claims continue valid. LIMITATIONS OF ACTIONS: Upon actions not in writing, three years; actions upon agreements, contracts, and promises in writing, five years. Judgments become dormant five years after the date of their rendition, or of the last execution issued thereon. A dormant judgment must be revived within one year after it has become dormant, or the right to revive is gone. LEGAL INTEREST, six per cent. EXEMPTIONS: A homestead, to the extent of one hundred and sixty acres of farming land, or one acre within the limits of an incorporated town or city, occupied as a residence by the family of the owner, together with all improvements on the same, shall be exempt from forced sale under any process of law, and shall not be alienated except by joint consent of husband and wife, when that relation exists. Not exempt, however, for taxes, or purchase-money obligations, or liens for improvements. No value is affixed to the homestead. It may be worth a million dollars. Earnings necessary for the support of the debtor's family are also exempted, and certain specified articles.

KENTUCKY.—Voluntary assignments by debtors must be made for the benefit of all creditors. Any creditor not presenting his claim within due time will be barred, unless otherwise ordered by the court. LIMITATION OF ACTIONS: Actions upon merchant's accounts for goods sold to consumers shall be brought in two years, the time to be computed from the first day of January next after the goods are sold and charged.

Actions upon contract, express or implied, not in writing, or bills of exchange, drafts, or upon a promissory note placed on the footing of a bill of exchange, or upon accounts between merchants or their agents, must be brought within five years. Actions upon judgments or contracts in writing must be brought within fifteen years. EXEMPTIONS: There is a homestead exemption of $1,000 to an actual, *bona fide*, resident housekeeper; with certain articles of personal property, and wages not to exceed fifty dollars, to persons who work for wages, under certain conditions. LEGAL INTEREST, six per cent.

LOUISIANA.—This State does not permit assignments of any sort, but it has an insolvent law, under which, by consent of a majority in number and amount of his creditors, a debtor may obtain his discharge, except as to those out of the State, and to these the State courts are closed to suits against the insolvent debtor. EXEMPTIONS: Homestead under certain conditions, specified articles, laborers' wages, etc. LIMITATIONS OF ACTIONS: Prescription of three years on all accounts, money lent, etc. This prescription only ceases from the time there has been an account acknowledged *in writing*, a note or bond given, or an action commenced. Five years—actions on bills of exchange and promissory notes, or rescission of contracts. Ten years—all judgments for money; may be revived at any time before prescription has run. Thirty years—all actions for immovable property. LEGAL INTEREST, five per cent.

MAINE.—Has an insolvency law, which does not permit preferences, but provides for the discharge of a debtor who is for the first time insolvent. Those who do not come into the assignment, should one be made, lose their dividends, but creditors who are not residents of the State may still enforce their claims. LIMITATIONS OF ACTIONS: All actions of debt, founded on contracts not under seal, must be commenced within six years after cause of action accrues ; judgments and witnessed promissory notes, twenty years. EXEMPTIONS: By complying with certain statutory provisions (not often taken advantage of), there is exempted a lot of land, dwelling-house, etc., not exceeding five hundred dollars in value—besides specified articles. LEGAL INTEREST, six per cent. Any rate may be fixed by contract.

MARYLAND.—Has a State insolvency law, which permits an assignment with preferences, under certain conditions. The debtor may obtain his discharge under the provisions of this law, but it is a nullity against non-resident creditors, unless they waive their right by voluntarily becoming parties to, and claiming under the insolvency proceedings. LIMITATIONS OF ACTIONS: Accounts and notes are barred after three years. Sealed instruments and judgments after twelve years. A verbal promise will revive a debt barred by the Statute of Limitations. EXEMPTIONS: One hundred dollars' worth of property is exempt, and, in addition thereto, all wearing apparel, books, and the tools of mechanics, except books or tools kept for sale. LEGAL INTEREST, six per cent.

MASSACHUSETTS.—Has a separate and distinct insolvent law. The debtor is not allowed to make a preferential assignment unless made six months before the filing of the petition in insolvency. The debtor may obtain his discharge if his assets pay fifty per cent of the claims proved ; otherwise, assent in writing of majority in number and value of creditors who have proved is necessary. Claims not proved are barred, unless creditors are non-residents. LIMITATIONS OF AC-TIONS : Accounts and actions of contract (excepting action brought upon a promissory note, signed in the presence of an attesting witness), six years. Judgments and actions, not specially otherwise limited, twenty years. EXEMPTIONS : Homestead of a householder having a family, to the value of eight hundred dollars, if he has duly declared his design to hold it as a homestead, and recorded it in compliance with the law ; besides other specified articles. LEGAL INTEREST, six per cent.

MICHIGAN.—There is in this State an assignment law. Preferences are forbidden. The debtor cannot obtain his discharge without unanimous consent of his creditors. Those who do not come into the assignment within ninety days, and prove their claims, lose their share of the assets assigned. LIMITATIONS OF ACTIONS : Six years on accounts and notes ; justices' judgments, six years. Sealed instruments, and judgments of courts of record, ten years. EXEMPTIONS : Land not exceeding forty acres, dwelling, and improvements in the country ; or land not exceeeding one lot in town or city, with dwelling, etc., owned and occupied by a resident of the State, to the value of fifteen hundred dollars; also specified articles. LEGAL INTEREST, six per cent.

MINNESOTA.—Has an assignment law, which does not permit preferences. LIMITATIONS : All actions on contracts, express or implied, must be commenced within six years. Judgments, ten years. EXEMPTIONS : Homestead, consisting of not to exceed eighty acres of land, with dwelling and appurtenances, in the country ;

14

or one lot, with dwelling, in a town or city having over
five thousand inhabitants, or one-half acre in a town or
village having less than five thousand inhabitants, and
dwelling, with appurtenances, owned and occupied by
any resident of the State. LEGAL INTEREST, ten per
cent.

MISSISSIPPI.—A distinct assignment law exists,
which went into operation with the adoption of the
new code, in the fall of 1892. It permits preferences,
but acceptance of a dividend from an estate under assignment does not discharge the debtor. Those who do
not come in get no distributive share. EXEMPTIONS:
Homestead land, not to exceed one hundred and sixty
acres, with buildings, owned and occupied as a residence,
not exceeding two thousand dollars in value. This may
be increased to three thousand dollars, by making and
recording a homestead declaration. There are numerous other specified exemptions of implements and personal property. LIMITATIONS OF ACTIONS: Accounts and
all unwritten contracts, three years; notes, bonds, etc.,
six years; judgments, seven years. Partial payments
do not stop the running of limitations. LEGAL INTER-
EST, six per cent.

MISSOURI.—Has an assignment law, preferences not
permitted. Debtor is not discharged without consent
of his creditors. Acceptance of dividend does not prevent creditor from placing balance of his claim in judgment. LIMITATIONS OF ACTIONS: On accounts, five years;
notes and sealed instruments, ten years; judgments,
ten years. EXEMPTIONS: Homestead of resident, married man, with varying quantity of land, according to
locality in the country, or in town or city according to
population, not to exceed in value fifteen hundred dol-

lars. Personal property or real estate, to the amount of not less than three hundred dollars; with tools, furniture, etc., as specified. LEGAL INTEREST, six per cent.

MONTANA.—Assignments may be made at common law, with preferences. Acceptance of a dividend from an estate under assignment does not discharge the debtor. Those who do not come in lose their dividends. LIMITATIONS OF ACTIONS: Upon accounts, five years; note, or written obligation, eight years; judgments, ten years. EXEMPTIONS: To married men, or the head of a family, homestead, not to exceed in value twenty-five hundred dollars, with other specified exemptions; none of the personal property is exempt for the wages of any clerk, mechanic, laborer, or servant. LEGAL INTEREST, ten per cent.

NEBRASKA.—Has a distinct assignment law, which does not permit preferences, and acceptance of a dividend does not discharge the debtor. Those who do not come in merely lose their distributive share of the assets. LIMITATIONS OF ACTIONS: Actions upon specific written contracts, or foreign judgments, must be brought within five years; actions upon contracts not in writing, four years. EXEMPTIONS: Homestead with dwelling thereon and its appurtenances, all not over two thousand dollars in value, to the head of a family. Heads of families, who have neither lands nor houses subject to exemption as a homestead, shall have exempt from forced sale on execution, the sum of five hundred dollars in personal property. Other exemptions of specified articles, etc. LEGAL INTEREST, seven per cent.

NEVADA.—Has "an act for the relief of insolvent debtors and protection of creditors"—does not permit preferences. By giving up all his property, and mentioning all his creditors, with amounts due them, etc., in his schedule, the debtor may obtain his discharge. LIMITATIONS OF ACTIONS: Upon contract, obligation or liability not founded upon an instrument in writing, within four years; if founded upon an instrument in writing, five years; judgments, six years. EXEMPTIONS: Homestead, not exceeding five thousand dollars in value, for the head of a family, and other specified exemptions. LEGAL INTEREST, ten per cent.

NEW HAMPSHIRE.—Has assignment law; permits no preferences. If debtor's estate pays seventy per cent, he is entitled to a discharge. If less than seventy per cent, he can be discharged only on written consent of three-quarters in number and amount of his creditors. LIMITATIONS OF ACTIONS: Accounts and simple promissory notes, six years after maturity. Judgments, sealed instruments, and notes secured by mortgage of real estate, twenty years. EXEMPTIONS: Homestead, to the value of five hundred dollars, with specified articles. LEGAL INTEREST, six per cent.

NEW JERSEY.—Has an insolvent law, which affects only persons imprisoned for debt under it; the debtor's body may be released from imprisonment, but claims are not released. The debtor may make an assignment of his property for the benefit of his creditors, but without preferences. Claims not due receive dividends, less a reasonable rebate of interest; failure of the creditor to file his claim before distribution of the assets bars him from receiving his share of the dividends. Creditors who have presented their claims are barred from afterward bringing suit against the debtor upon them, unless fraud is proved. Outside of this law, a debtor may prefer any of his creditors by conveying his property to them. He may also, at any time before judgment and execution, sell, for a sufficient consideration, property which would otherwise be subject to the claims of his creditors. EXEMPTIONS : Property to the value of two hundred dollars, exclusive of wearing apparel. LIMITATIONS : Accounts, notes, and contracts, not under seal, six years ; bonds and other sealed instruments, sixteen years ; judgments, twenty years. LEGAL INTEREST, six per cent.

NEW MEXICO.—Has a voluntary assignment act. The proceedings are very elaborate. Preferences not allowed ; acceptance of a dividend does not discharge debtor. Those who do not come in lose their dividends. LIMITATIONS : Unwritten contracts, four years. Written instruments and judgments, seven years. EXEMPTIONS : Homestead, to the value of one thousand dollars, furniture, and specified articles. LEGAL INTEREST, six per cent.

NEW YORK.—Has both an assignment and an insolvent law ; The latter sometimes called the " Two-third Act." The debtor may make a preferential assignment, under certain limitations and conditions, or he may obtain a discharge from certain classes of his obligations under the insolvent law, without the unanimous consent of his creditors. Acceptance of a dividend under the assignment does not discharge the debtor. Creditors who do not come into the assignment lose their dividends, but retain their claims. EXEMPTIONS : The lot and buildings, not exceeding one thousand dollars in value, owned and occupied by a housekeeper, having a family, and recorded as homestead property ; with furniture and various articles, not exceeding two hun-

14

dred and fifty dollars in value. LIMITATIONS : Actions upon a judgment of a court of record, or a sealed instrument, must be brought within twenty years after the cause of action accrued. And upon any other contract, obligation or liability, including a justice's judgment, within six years. LEGAL INTEREST, six per cent.

NORTH CAROLINA.—Assignments may be made, without preferences. All debts of assignor fall due and are payable on the date of assignment. EXEMPTIONS : Homestead, with buildings, etc., to the value of one thousand dollars, and personal property to the value of five hundred dollars. LIMITATIONS : Three years, on accounts and contracts, not under seal; ten years, on a note under seal. LEGAL INTEREST, six per cent.

NORTH DAKOTA.—Insolvent debtor may make an assignment for the benefit of his creditors, but without preferences. EXEMPTIONS : Homestead, with dwelling and appurtenances, not exceeding in value five thousand dollars, is exempt, under certain conditions. A partnership firm or an individual may also, in addition to wearing apparel, etc., claim as exempt fifteen hundred dollars' worth of other personal property. LIMITATIONS : On judgments, or on sealed instruments, twenty years ; on a contract, obligation, or liability, express or implied, six years. LEGAL INTEREST, seven per cent.

OHIO.—Has a distinct assignment law, which does not permit preferences. Acceptance of a dividend does not discharge the debtor. Creditors who do not come in receive no dividend. LIMITATIONS : Actions upon a contract not in writing, six years; upon a sealed instrument, or an agreement, contract, or promise in writing, fifteen years; judgment is dormant if no execution is issued within five years after its date. An action to revive dormant judgment must be brought within twenty-one years after it becomes dormant. EXEMP-TIONS: To head of a family, homestead, not exceeding one thousand dollars in value, and chattel property. If not the owner of a homestead—personal property to the value of five hundred dollars, in addition to chattel property. LEGAL INTEREST, six per cent.

OKLAHOMA TERRITORY.—Assignments may be made for the benefit of creditors, without preferences. LIMITATIONS: Accounts and contracts, not in writing, three years; agreement or contract in writing, five years. EXEMPTIONS: To head of a family, one hundred and sixty acres in one tract, with improvements, if outside of a town or city. In a city or town, not to exceed one acre. Judgment debtor has a right to select six hundred dollars' worth of property, which shall be exempt from any levy. LEGAL INTEREST, seven per cent.

OREGON.—Assignments must be for the equal benefit of all creditors, without preferences. Debtor is entitled to a discharge, if his estate pays fifty per cent to his creditors. LIMITATIONS: Judgments, ten years. Action upon a contract or liability, express or implied, six years. EXEMPTIONS: Homestead, not exceeding in value fifteen hundred dollars, with chattels. LEGAL INTEREST, eight per cent.

PENNSYLVANIA.—Insolvent may make a voluntary general assignment for the benefit of his creditors, without preferences. But the debtor can do in other ways what substantially amounts to a preferential assignment, viz., before he makes his general assignment, he may assign part of his property to one or more creditors; or he may confess judgment, under which the favored creditor may make a levy, and obtain priority. Creditors who do not come into the assignment simply fail to get their share, their claims remain intact. LIMITATIONS : Notes and accounts, six years ; judgments and instruments under seal, twenty years, by presumption, but this presumption may be rebutted. EXEMPTIONS : Things of domestic use, to the value of three hundred dollars. LEGAL INTEREST, six per cent.

RHODE ISLAND.—Has no distinct assignment or insolvent law, but debtor may make an assignment ; preferences are forbid, except for the wages of labor, performed within six months previous. Judgment by default, or confession, cannot be made to defeat general creditors. Acceptance of a dividend does not discharge the debtor, nor does he obtain such discharge, without the unanimous consent of his creditors. Those who do not come into the assignment lose their share of the dividends. LIMITATIONS : Accounts, six years ; simple promissory notes, six years ; sealed instruments and judgments, twenty years. Oral promise, or partial payment, will revive the debt. EXEMPTIONS : There is no homestead exemption. Household furniture and family stores of housekeeper are exempt, to the value of three hundred dollars, with wearing apparel, etc. Debts secured by promissory notes or bills of exchange are also exempt. LEGAL INTEREST, six per cent.

SOUTH CAROLINA.—There is in this State a law for the relief of persons arrested in civil actions ; undue preferences are forbidden. A discharge releases the insolvent from all suing creditors, and from all other creditors who shall come in and accept a dividend of the assigned effects. The debt due to a creditor is not affected if he does not participate in the dividends. LIMITATIONS : Judgments and sealed instruments, twenty years; other actions, six years. EXEMPTIONS : Family homestead of the head of family, to the value of one thousand dollars, and yearly produce thereof; also to head of family, certain goods and chattels, to the value of five hundred dollars. LEGAL INTEREST, seven per cent.

SOUTH DAKOTA.—An insolvent debtor may execute an assignment of property to one or more assignees, in trust, toward the satisfaction of his creditors ; but such assignment shall not be valid, if it contain any trust or condition by which any creditor is to receive a preference over any other creditor. LIMITATIONS : Sealed instruments, twenty years; judgments, ten years; notes and contracts, express or implied, six years. EXEMPTIONS : Homestead, with improvements thereon, not exceeding in value five thousand dollars ; domestic goods and chattels specified ; and, to head of family, the right to select seven hundred and fifty dollars' worth of other personal property, under certain conditions. If a single person, three hundred dollars' worth. LEGAL INTEREST, seven per cent.

TENNESSEE.—Has two general classes of assignments, namely : (1) General assignments, which are the creatures of statute, are very technical, and have been practically abandoned. Attempt to prefer creditors renders a general assignment fraudulent. (2) Partial assignments, which may include all of the debtor's property if it does not profess to do so. In this form of assignment, preferences may be made. Creditors not included in partial or "special" assignments have no remedy, except by reaching property of the assignor not included in the instrument, or by having the assignment set aside, provided, of course, there be grounds for such action. LIMITATIONS: Judgments, ten years. (There are no sealed instruments in Tennessee). Notes and accounts, six years. EXEMPTIONS: Homestead, to the value of one thousand dollars, and a long list of specified articles. LEGAL INTEREST, six per cent.

TEXAS.—Has an assignment law, which does not permit preferences; but these can be made under a deed of trust, which is now the course pursued by insolvent debtors. Acceptance of a dividend from an estate under assignment discharges debtor if total dividends amount to one-third of creditor's claims. Those who do not come into an assignment lose their dividends, but preserve their claims. LIMITATIONS: Accounts, two years; notes, four years; judgments, ten years. EXEMPTIONS: Homestead occupied as a home, or as a place to exercise the calling or business of the head of a family, to the value of five thousand dollars without reference to the value of any improvements thereon; also, specified goods and chattels. LEGAL INTEREST, six per cent.

UTAH.—No separate, distinct assignment, insolvency, or bankrupt law exists in this Territory; but the debtor is permitted by law to make an assignment, with preferences; but he cannot obtain a discharge without the unanimous consent of creditors, who lose their dividends, but preserve their claims, if they do not come in. LIMITATIONS: Accounts, two years; notes and written obligations, four years; judgments of a court of record, five years. EXEMPTIONS: (No property owned by nonresidents is exempt.) If the debtor is the head of a family, there is exempt, homestead, valued at one thousand dollars, five hundred additional for wife, and two hundred and fifty for each other member of the family; besides goods and chattels specified. LEGAL INTEREST, eight per cent.

VERMONT.—Has insolvency laws, both voluntary and involuntary. Insolvent debtor is not allowed to make preferential assignment. When his assets pay thirty per cent, or by vote of majority in number and amount of his creditors, debtor is discharged. Second discharge, only by payment of fifty per cent, or, by vote of three-fourths in number and amount, of his creditors. Foreign creditors, who do not submit to the jurisdiction of the insolvency court, may recover judgment against the debtor, notwithstanding his discharge in insolvency. LIMITATIONS: Accounts and simple promissory notes are barred in six years. Notes signed in presence of an attesting witness, fourteen years. Sealed instruments and judgments, eight years. EXEMPTIONS: Homestead, to the value of five hundred dollars, and products, with specified goods and chattels. LEGAL INTEREST, six per cent.

VIRGINIA.—Has no separate and distinct assignment, insolvency, or bankrupt law. But the debtor can make a preferential assignment. The unanimous consent of creditors is required for the discharge of the debtor. Creditors who do not come into the assignment lose their dividends, but preserve their claims. LIMITATIONS: Five years on accounts, (except for articles charged in retail stores, which is two years) ; notes and contracts, five years; sealed instruments, ten years. Judgments ten years (in some cases twenty years). EXEMPTIONS: Householder or head of a family may hold exempt his real and personal property, or either, including money or debts due him, to a value not exceeding two thousand dollars, to be selected by him, with certain specified articles. Intention to claim such homestead exemption must be declared and recorded. LEGAL INTEREST, six per cent.

WASHINGTON.—Has an insolvent law. General assignment of a debtor must be for the benefit of all his creditors, in proportion to the amount of their claims, and when the requirements of the law are complied with, the debtor is discharged from further liability. LIMITATIONS: Upon contracts not in writing, three years. Upon judgments, or contracts in writing, six years. EXEMPTIONS: Homestead, with numerous specified articles, and special exemptions. LEGAL INTEREST, seven per cent.

WEST VIRGINIA.—General assignments can be made, without preferences. Unanimous consent of creditors required for debtor's discharge. Acceptance of a dividend from the assignee does not discharge debtor. Creditors who do not come into an assignment do not impair their rights of action, and there is no reason why they should refuse to accept their dividends. LIMITATIONS: Accounts, five years (except articles charged in a store account, which is three years) ; contracts under seal, ten years; judgments, ten years. EXEMPTIONS: Homestead, to the value of one thousand dollars, to a husband or parent, if declaration is previously made and recorded ; also to husband, parent, or married woman, personal property to the value of two hundred dollars ; also tools of a mechanic or laborer, to the value of fifty dollars. LEGAL INTEREST, six per cent.

WISCONSIN.—Has both an assignment and an insolvency law. Preferences are not permitted, except for wages earned within six months. Under the insolvent law, all debts are discharged. LIMITATIONS : Accounts, six years; notes, six years; sealed instruments, ten years, when the cause of action accrued without the State and twenty years when it accrued within the State; twenty years upon a judgment within the State, and ten years on a judgment recovered out of the State. EXEMPTIONS : Homestead in the country, used for agricultural purposes, with dwelling-house thereon, and appurtenances, or, at the option of the owner, land (with dwelling, etc.) not to exceed one-fourth of an acre, in a city or village; with various other specified exemptions. LEGAL INTEREST, six per cent.

WYOMING.—Has an assignment law, which is void, if made with a view to preferring a creditor. Acceptance of a dividend from an estate under assignment discharges the debtor. Creditors who do not come into an assignment lose their dividends, but preserve their rights of subsequent action. LIMITATIONS : Action on any agreement in writing, five years; on actions on accounts, and contracts not in writing, eight years; on all foreign claims, judgments, or contracts contracted or incurred before the debtor becomes a resident, action shall be commenced within two years after established residence. EXEMPTIONS : Homestead occupied by owner or his family, not exceeding in value fifteen hundred dollars; household property, owned by the head of a family, to the value of five hundred dollars; other specified exemptions for mechanics, miners, etc. LEGAL INTEREST, eight per cent.

www.ingramcontent.com/pod-product-compliance
Lightning Source LLC
Chambersburg PA
CBHW030130030726
47498CB00007B/2629